RELATED STUDIES for use with this book _____

WORLD CULTURES* books include:

(Dual editions)

MAN IN EUROPE—BRITISH ISLES AND GERMANY, 1972
MAN IN EUROPE—FRANCE AND SOVIET UNION, 1972
MAN IN ASIA—INDIA AND SOUTHEAST ASIA, 1972
MAN IN AFRICA AND SOUTH AMERICA, 1972

(Individual studies)

BRITISH ISLES, 1972       GERMANY, 1972
FRANCE, 1972              SOVIET UNION, 1972
INDIA, 1972               SOUTHEAST ASIA, 1972
AFRICA, 1972              SOUTH AMERICA, 1972

MAN IN THE UNITED STATES*

THE NORTHEAST, 1972
THE SOUTH, 1971
MIDWEST AND GREAT PLAINS, 1972
THE WEST, 1972

MAN IN CANADA AND LATIN AMERICA

CANADA, 1972
MEXICO, 1971
SOUTH AMERICA, 1972
CARIBBEAN LANDS, 1972

MAN IN EUROPE

ITALY, 1971
NETHERLANDS, 1970
SPAIN, 1970
SWITZERLAND, 1971

*Teacher's Guide is available

THE FIDELER COMPANY  31 Ottawa, N.W., Grand Rapids, Michigan  49502

# SOUTH AMERICA

Raymond E. Fideler

Raymond E. Fideler is a nationally known editor and publisher of social studies textbooks. He is a graduate of Drake University. Through extensive travel, he has gained firsthand knowledge of the countries of South America.

Carol Kvande

Carol Kvande received her education at Upsala College and the University of Illinois. As a former teacher, Mrs. Kvande is keenly aware of the needs and interests of students. She has made a special study of the land and the people of South America.

THE FIDELER COMPANY Grand Rapids, Michigan / Toronto, Canada

# SOUTH AMERICA

## CONTRIBUTORS

**AROLDO DE AZEVEDO**
Professor of Geography
São Paulo University
São Paulo, Brazil

**G. ETZEL PEARCY**
Chairman, Department
of Geography
California State College
Los Angeles, California

**JAVIER ENRIQUE SOMOZA**
Professor of Geography
Salvador University
Buenos Aires, Argentina

**ROBERT H. BAUER**
Art Director

**BRONWYN MEGAN HARRIS**
Manuscript Editor

**DEBORAH J. BOLT**
Picture Editor

**MARY MITUS**
Map Editor

**RAYMOND E. FIDELER**
Editor and President

**BEV J. ROCHE**
Design Editor

**MARIANNE FRIEDL**
Map Supervisor

**MARY JANE SACK**
Staff Writer

**AUDREY WITHAM**
Manuscript Editor

**Threshing grain in Peru.** About 195 million people make their homes in South America. More than half of them earn their living by farming.

# CONTENTS

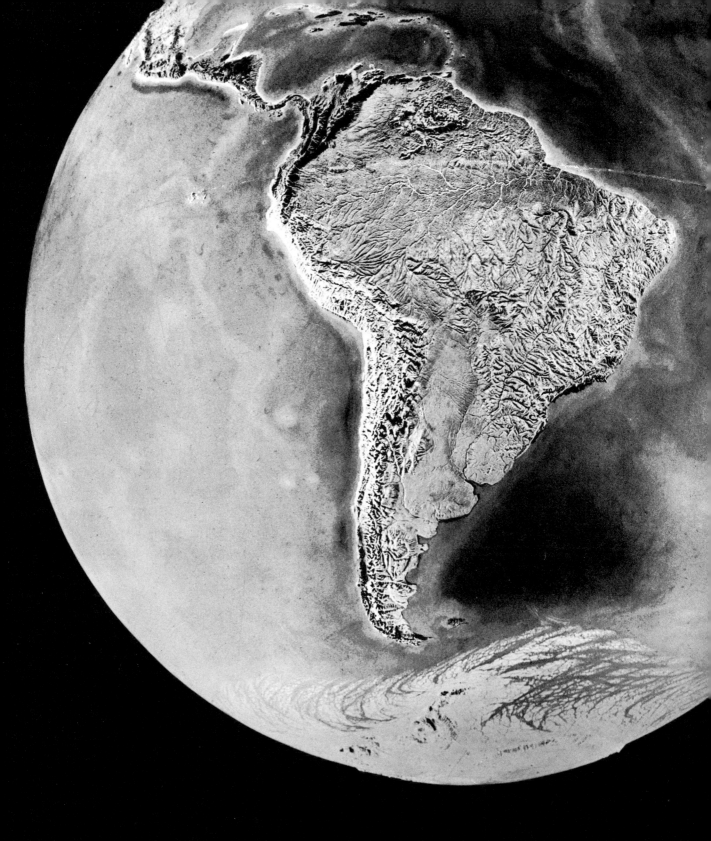

SOUTH AMERICA

## An Overview of South America

**A huge land of great variety.** The map on page 9 shows South America, our neighbor continent in the Western Hemisphere.* This continent covers an area nearly twice the size of the United States. On such a large landmass it is not surprising to find many kinds of land features. A visitor to South America will see towering mountains and deep valleys, fertile plains and swampy lowlands. He will also find great variety in climate. Some parts of South America receive more than one hundred inches of rainfall a year. In other places, years may pass without a drop of rain. The rainforest of South America is always hot and humid, while the highest mountain peaks are covered with a blanket of snow the year around.

**The home of many different peoples.** The first people to make their homes on the continent of South America were Indians who came here thousands of years ago. About A.D. 1500, people from Spain and Portugal began coming to South America. They conquered most of the Indians and established colonies. Later, some of the settlers brought Negro slaves from Africa to work in mines and on plantations. As the years passed, many of these different peoples intermarried.* During the 1800's and early 1900's, millions of people came to South America from Germany, Italy, Great Britain, and other European countries. Others came

*See Glossary

**South American Indians** near the city of La Paz, Bolivia. Many different peoples live on the vast continent of South America.

A view of Lima, Peru. Many South Americans have moved into cities in recent years. What are some of the problems this has created? How are most South American governments trying to solve these problems?

from Asian lands such as Japan, China, and Syria. The descendants of all these different peoples live in South America today. In addition, people are still coming to South America from other parts of the world.

**Important changes have taken place in South America in recent years.** During the past twenty years, great changes have affected the lives of people in South America. Many thousands of South Americans have moved from rural areas into the cities. In addition, the governments of many countries have taken over certain mines and processing plants on the continent. New social and political organizations have also brought changes to South America. These new organizations are helping many South Americans

to participate more effectively in their communities.

**Many South Americans have moved into the cities in search of a better way of life.** During the days when South America was made up largely of colonies belonging to Portugal and Spain, most of the farmland there was divided into large estates. Many of these estates still exist today. Because they take up so much farmland, there has been little good land left for other people to farm. Most farmers in South America who own land have only small plots on which to grow crops. Many of these farmers are not able to raise enough food for their families. Other South Americans own no land at all. They must work as laborers on the large estates. Because they are paid very low

dreds of thousands of them have been moving into South America's cities in search of a better way of life. For example, the populations of Lima, Peru, and Caracas, Venezuela, have both increased by nearly one million in the past ten years.

The rapid increase in urban population has created many problems in South America. The overcrowded cities do not have adequate housing, schools, and hospitals for all the people. In many cities, there are densely populated slum areas that lack electricity and running water. Most of the new city dwellers do not have the skills that would enable them to get jobs in business and industry. Many cannot even read and write. As a result, thousands of city dwellers are unable to find any way of earning a living.

The governments of most South American countries are trying to find ways to solve these problems. They are trying to provide low-cost housing, improve education, and encourage the development of industry. They are also looking for ways to open up new land for settlement and to make better use of their countries' natural resources.

In Brazil, for example, the government is now constructing a road through the Amazon Lowland. When this road is completed, it will connect cities along Brazil's Atlantic coast with cities more than two thousand miles away along the country's western border. This new road will provide an important transportation route through a vast, underdeveloped area that makes up the northern half of Brazil. Towns and cities will be built along this road to provide new homes for many of the people who now live in

wages, they find it difficult to meet their needs.

About twenty years ago, some South American governments began trying to solve this problem. They began to buy many of the large estates. They distributed the land from these estates among many of the poor farm families. This distribution of land is known as land reform. Today, nearly every South American country has a land reform program. Thousands of families in Bolivia, Chile, Venezuela, and Colombia have been given their own land to farm.

In spite of land reform, however, millions of rural families in South America are not able to meet their needs. Above all, they are not able to obtain enough food to eat. Partly because of this, hun-

Brazil's crowded slums. Farms will be established on land opened up along both sides of the new road. Mining companies will be able to use the road to reach the Amazon Lowland's rich mineral deposits, which include one of the world's largest deposits of iron ore.

**The governments of some South American countries have been taking over mines and processing plants.** At about the same time that many land reform programs were started in South America, some people were becoming dissatisfied over the ways in which the continent's natural resources were being used. During the past one hundred years, many mines and processing plants had been established in South America by businessmen from the United States and other parts of the world. Others had been established by wealthy South Americans. The owners of these mines and processing plants often took the profits from their South American businesses and deposited them in banks in other parts of the world. This made many South Americans dissatisfied because they felt that the profits should be used to benefit the people of South America. Partly because of this, the governments of some South American countries have taken over, or nationalized, certain mines and plants in recent years. The huge tin mines in Bolivia were nationalized in the early 1950's. In other South American countries, the governments have nationalized the production of petroleum, copper, zinc, and other minerals.

The nationalization of mines and processing plants seems to have benefited some of the people in South America. It has given many people a new sense of pride in their government. It has also helped some of them to achieve a higher standard* of living. For example, wages for Peruvian mine workers have doubled since Peru's copper and zinc mines were nationalized.

The nationalization of mines and plants has led to some problems, however. In Chile, for example, production in the mines decreased when they were taken over by the government. Also, some South American governments have nationalized mines and plants without paying the owners any money in return. This has made some businessmen re-

luctant to invest in the new mines and factories that are needed on the continent. It has even led to unfriendly relations between some South American countries and the United States.

**New social and political organizations are bringing changes to South America.** Until recently, few South Americans took part in government. Some countries came to be ruled by military dictators who ignored the results of national elections. The leaders of some countries would not allow the people to choose

their own local officials. Even people who had the right to vote often did not do so. Probably fewer than 20 percent of the people took part in elections. Because many South Americans could not or would not participate in government, they began to feel they could do little to improve their lives.

In recent years, however, new political organizations have been formed. Through these organizations, more people in South America are taking an active part in government. They are

A political demonstration in Chile. Chile has several political parties. These include the Communist Party, whose symbol is shown below. Do research in other sources to discover some of the functions of a political party in a democracy such as Chile or the United States.

working together to demand land reform and other changes from their government leaders. In addition, community groups and labor unions have been formed to work for changes that will benefit the people of South America.

One country in which several new organizations have been formed recently is Peru. For many years, the Indian people of Peru have been electing their own leaders in a democratic way. The Indian people also have a long history of cooperating with one another in order to farm their lands and to build houses, roads, and schools.

During the past fifteen years, many of these Indian people have left their homes in the harsh climate of the high Andes Mountains to settle in the cities along Peru's Pacific coast. They have built whole new communities of straw mat or adobe houses in the open areas of land on the edges of the cities. The Indian people have worked together to build meetinghouses and roads for their new communities. They have formed groups to work for such things as better housing and a greater voice in government.

The government leaders in Peru have been very much impressed by the accomplishments of the Indian people. They admire the way these people work together to improve their way of life. Some of the ways in which the Indians have cooperated with one another have been adopted by the country as a whole. A national program called Community Action has been established by the government to give funds to communities whose people will work together to build roads, buildings, and irrigation projects.

**The people of South America are learning to cooperate.** Many people in South America today are developing a new feeling about their countries and about the continent as a whole. They are beginning to think of themselves as Latin Americans. People in many South American countries are beginning to realize that they have much in common with people living in other parts of the continent. They know, too, that they have much in common with people in the United States. They are learning that they can help solve their problems and improve their lives through cooperation.

One important way in which the countries of South America have been cooperating with each other is in reaching agreements about trade. Most South American countries belong to the Latin American Free Trade Association. This organization is trying to promote trade among its members by reducing taxes and tariffs on goods that one country sells to another. Five South American countries have also signed the Andean Pact, an agreement to promote further trade and cooperation.

The South American countries are cooperating in other ways as well. Some countries are providing money to help their less wealthy neighbors. In addition, South American nations are working together on projects that will help make better use of each country's natural resources. For example, Argentina, Bolivia, Brazil, Paraguay, and Uruguay have formed the Río de la Plata Basin Organization. The members of this organization have agreed to make a study of the river basin's natural resources and to cooperate with one another in development projects.

CARIBBEAN SEA

Aruba (Neth.)
Curaçao (Neth.)
Trinidad
Barranquilla
ISTHMUS OF PANAMA
Maracaibo
Lake Maracaibo
Caracas
VENEZUELA
GUYANA
Paramaribo
Georgetown
FRENCH GUIANA
Cayenne
SURINAM (Neth.)
Medellín
Bogotá
Cali
COLOMBIA
Orinoco R.
ATLANTIC
Equator
Quito
ECUADOR
Río Negro
Amazon R.
Pará R.
OCEAN
Guayaquil
Belém
Amazon R.
Fortaleza
ANDES MTS.
PERU
Purús R.
Madeira R.
Tapajoz R.
Marañón R.
B R A Z I L
Recife
Lima
Xingú R.
Araguaia R.
Tocantins R.
São Francisco R.
O C E A N
Beni R.
Lake Titicaca
La Paz
BOLIVIA
Salvador
Sucre
Brasília
Belo Horizonte
PARAGUAY
Paraguay R.
Tropic of Capricorn
São Paulo
Rio de Janeiro
Asunción
Curitiba
Paraná R.
ANDES MOUNTAINS
CHILE
ARGENTINA
Córdoba
Pôrto Alegre
Mt. Aconcagua
URUGUAY
Paraná R.
Uruguay R.
Rosario
Montevideo
Santiago
Buenos Aires
Río de la Plata
Colorado R.
PACIFIC
ATLANTIC

SOUTH AMERICA

Miles
0 100 200 300 400

Cities
★ Capitals
□ 500,000 to 750,000
○ 750,000 and Over

Elevations in Feet

| | |
|---|---|
| | 15,000 and Over |
| | 10,000 to 15,000 |
| | 5,000 to 10,000 |
| | 1,000 to 5,000 |
| | 0 to 1,000 |

Miles
0 40 80

GALÁPAGOS ISLANDS (ECUA.)

FALKLAND ISLANDS
(Br., Claimed by Argentina)

CAPE HORN

9

# Part 1
# Land and Climate

The continent of South America is divided into thirteen countries and territories that have widely contrasting land features and varying climates. As you do research in Part 1 of this book, you will be able to discover facts about land and climate in South America and how they differ from one part of the continent to another. You may wish to use the following questions to guide your research.

- In which South American countries or territories would you find high mountains? dense rainforests? plateaus and hills? barren deserts? grasslands?
- Which country or territory in South America has land and climate most like the land and climate where you live?

In doing research, remember that maps and photographs provide valuable information about land and climate.

**Lake Nahuel Huapí,** in the Andes Mountains in Argentina. South America is a huge continent of contrasting land features and varying climates.

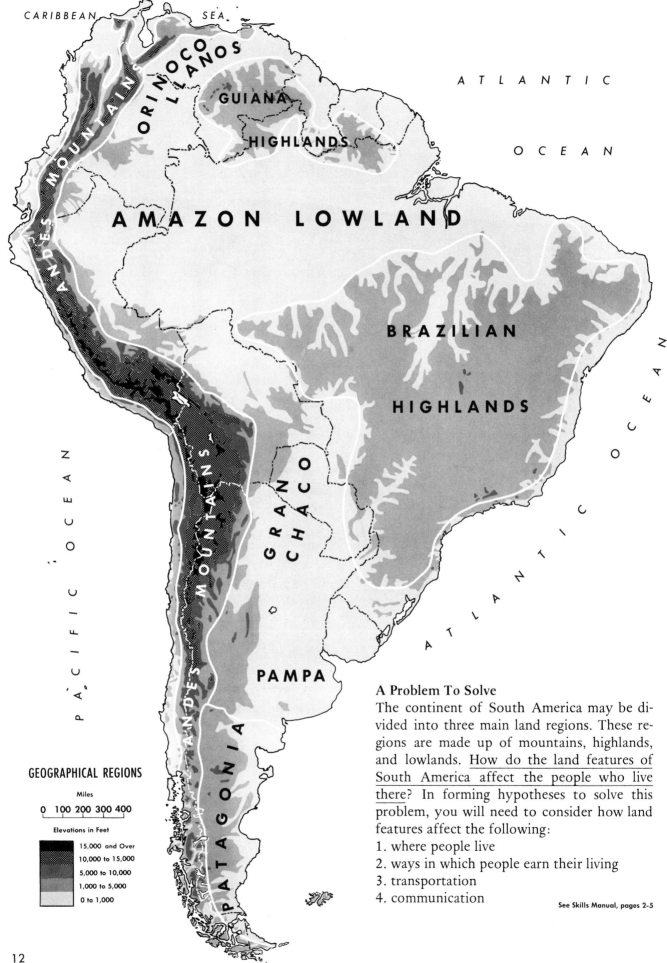

CARIBBEAN          SEA

ATLANTIC

OCEAN

ORINOCO LLANOS

GUIANA

HIGHLANDS

ANDES MOUNTAIN

AMAZON LOWLAND

BRAZILIAN

HIGHLANDS

PACIFIC OCEAN

ANDES MOUNTAINS

GRAN CHACO

ATLANTIC OCEAN

PAMPA

PATAGONIA

**GEOGRAPHICAL REGIONS**

Miles

0  100 200 300 400

Elevations in Feet

15,000 and Over

10,000 to 15,000

5,000 to 10,000

1,000 to 5,000

0 to 1,000

**A Problem To Solve**

The continent of South America may be divided into three main land regions. These regions are made up of mountains, highlands, and lowlands. How do the land features of South America affect the people who live there? In forming hypotheses to solve this problem, you will need to consider how land features affect the following:

1. where people live
2. ways in which people earn their living
3. transportation
4. communication

See Skills Manual, pages 2-5

12

**A high plateau in the Andes Mountains.** This rugged mountain chain makes up nearly one fifth of South America. In what ways do the Andes vary from the northern part of the continent to the southern part?

# 1 Land

The huge continent of South America may be divided into three main land regions. The first region is the towering mountain chain that stretches along the western coast of the continent. (See map on page 12.) The mountains in this chain are known as the Andes. Highlands in the northern, eastern, and southern parts of the continent form the second land region. The third region consists of the vast lowlands of South America.

**The mountain chain.** The Andes Mountains are the longest unbroken chain of mountains in the world. They extend about five thousand miles along the western coast of South America. (See map on page 12.) Altogether, they occupy almost one fifth of the continent.

The Andes differ greatly from north to south. In the southern part of the continent they are quite narrow. Here are beautiful lakes, gleaming snowfields, and sparkling glaciers. Farther north, many peaks rise more than twenty thousand feet above the level of the sea. In the central and northern Andes, the

mountains spread out into parallel ranges. Between these ranges are high plateaus and deep canyons. Some of the canyons are almost twice as deep as the Grand Canyon in the United States. Many of the plateaus are more than two miles above sea level. Nestled on one of these high plateaus is Lake Titicaca, one of the largest lakes in South America. (See map on page 9.) West of Lake Titicaca are huge cone-shaped volcanoes. Throughout the Andes there are many volcanoes like these. Some of them rumble and send out smoke and ashes. Sometimes, violent earthquakes shake the land. Nature is still at work changing this rugged region.

**Highlands of South America.** The second region of South America is made up of the Guiana Highlands, the Brazilian Highlands, and Patagonia. The plateaus, hills, and low mountains of these three main highland areas cover about one third of the continent of South America.

The Guiana Highlands are located in Venezuela, Guyana, Surinam, French Guiana, and northern Brazil. (See maps on pages 9 and 12.) This highland area does not have rugged peaks like the Andes Mountains. Here nature has worn the land down to form rounded hills, narrow valleys, and flat-topped table-lands. A small river plunges over the edge of one of these tablelands and

forms the highest waterfall in the world. This is Angel Falls in Venezuela. It is more than three thousand feet high—nearly twenty times the height of Niagara Falls in the United States.

The Brazilian Highlands cover a larger area than any other part of the highland region. (See map on page 12.) This highland area extends along the coast of Brazil for nearly two thousand miles. From the coast it stretches westward far into the interior of the continent. The Brazilian Highlands are made up of tablelands, rounded hills, and steep mountains. Most of the people of Brazil live in the eastern part of the Brazilian Highlands.

The third part of South America's highland region is Patagonia, in the southern part of the continent. Patagonia is a cool, dry plateau located between the Andes Mountains and the Atlantic Ocean. (See map on page 12.) Much of this upland area is barren and dry. At the western edge of Patagonia, however, there are many beautiful lakes, which were formed by glaciers thousands of years ago.

**Lowlands of South America.** The Amazon Lowland, in the northern part of the continent, is the largest lowland area in South America. (See map on page 12.) It is drained by the Amazon River and its tributaries.* This vast plain extends from the Andes Mountains to the

*See Glossary

**The city of Nova Friburgo,** in the Brazilian Highlands. The Brazilian Highlands form the largest part of South America's highland region. What are the other two main parts?

Atlantic Ocean, a distance of more than two thousand miles. In western Brazil, the Amazon Lowland extends about eight hundred miles from north to south. Much of the Amazon Lowland is covered with dense rainforest. Parts of it are open grasslands.

South of the Amazon Lowland lies another vast lowland, drained by three great rivers—the Paraguay, the Paraná, and the Uruguay. The northern part of the lowland is an area of grasslands and forests called the Gran Chaco. (See map on page 12.) The part of this lowland that lies in central Argentina is called the Pampa. The fertile Pampa is one of the most important agricultural areas in the world.

Between the Andes Mountains and the Guiana Highlands, in the northern part of South America, is another lowland called the Orinoco Llanos. (See map on page 12.) This is a flat grassland with low hills and scattered patches of trees. Very few people live in this part of the continent.

**In the Amazon Lowland,** near Belém, Brazil. The Amazon Lowland is the largest lowland area in South America. Much of this lowland is covered with dense rainforest. What facts help to explain why this is so? Chapter 2 contains information that will be helpful in answering this question.

**January in Buenos Aires, Argentina.** Lands south of the equator have summer rather than winter during the months of December, January, and February. What facts help to explain why this is so?

# 2  Climate

**It is summer in Buenos Aires when it is winter in Chicago.** On a cold day in January, we board a plane in Chicago to begin a jet flight to Buenos Aires. In Chicago, it is only ten degrees above zero. Snow is falling. The people at the airport are wearing heavy winter clothing.

The top map on page 18 shows the route we will take on our flight from Chicago to Buenos Aires. It also shows the zones of temperature through which we will travel. About thirty minutes after taking off from the Chicago airport, we leave the zone of cold winter weather. For over an hour, we fly above the zone of cool weather that covers

most of our southern states. Next, we fly over Florida, which lies in the zone of warm winter weather. Soon after leaving Florida, we are in the hot zone. The top map on page 18 shows that in January this zone of hot weather extends far into the southern part of the continent of South America.

About sixteen hours after leaving Chicago, we land at the busy airport in Buenos Aires. The sun is shining brightly on this January day, and we see that the people here are dressed in light summer clothes. It seems strange to us to carry the winter coats that we were wearing yesterday when we began our

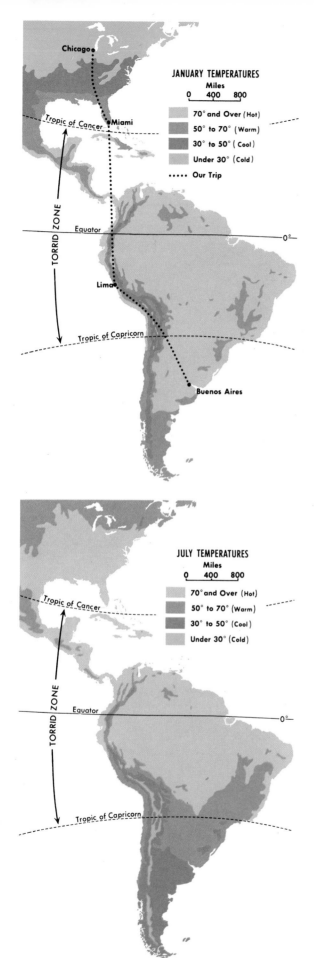

JANUARY TEMPERATURES

Miles
0    400    800

| | |
|---|---|
| | 70° and Over (Hot) |
| | 50° to 70° (Warm) |
| | 30° to 50° (Cool) |
| | Under 30° (Cold) |
| ••••• | Our Trip |

Chicago

Miami

Tropic of Cancer

TORRID ZONE

Equator                                        0°

Lima

Tropic of Capricorn

Buenos Aires

JULY TEMPERATURES

Miles
0    400    800

| | |
|---|---|
| | 70° and Over (Hot) |
| | 50° to 70° (Warm) |
| | 30° to 50° (Cool) |
| | Under 30° (Cold) |

Tropic of Cancer

TORRID ZONE

Equator                                        0°

Tropic of Capricorn

flight in Chicago. As we leave the plane, the stewardess tells us that the temperature outside is ninety degrees. It is summer in Buenos Aires.

The summer months in most of South America, as in other lands in the Southern Hemisphere,* are December, January, and February. During these months, lands south of the equator are tilted toward the sun and receive many hours

*See Glossary

**Copacabana Beach** in Rio de Janeiro, Brazil. In many parts of South America, the weather is warm enough for people to enjoy the beaches all year long. Why does much of this continent have a hot climate?

of warm sunshine. At the same time, lands in the Northern Hemisphere* are tilted away from the sun. There, days are shorter and the slanting rays of the sun bring less warmth to the land. In the Southern Hemisphere all four seasons of the year come at exactly the opposite times that these seasons occur in the Northern Hemisphere. In the Southern Hemisphere, summer begins in De-

cember, autumn in March, winter in June, and spring in September.

**Even in winter, much of South America has a hot climate.** The temperature maps on the opposite page show that the weather is hot all year round in much of South America. Even in July, which is a winter month south of the equator, the weather is hot in more than half the continent. The temperature maps help explain why this is true. We can see that the equator passes through the northern part of South America. The zone of hot lands near the equator, called the tropics, receives warm sunshine all year. Much of South America is in this zone, and therefore receives warm sunshine all year long.

**In the mountains and highlands, the climate is cooler.** The higher we go in the mountains or the highlands, the cooler the air becomes. Each three to four hundred feet of altitude makes a difference of one degree of temperature. Even near the equator, there are peaks in the Andes so high that they are always covered with snow. Let's take a trip in the Andes, so that we can pass through several kinds of climate in a single day.

**A train trip in the Andes.** We begin our trip at Guayaquil, Ecuador's chief port. This city is near the equator. Here the weather is always hot. As we travel eastward across the broad valley in which Guayaquil is located, we see fields of sugarcane and rice. Soon we reach the foothills of the Andes Mountains. We pass banana and cacao* plantations. As our train climbs in the mountains, we notice that the air is not quite so hot as it was in the valley. By the time the train has reached five thousand feet above sea level, the air is pleasantly cool. We see fields of wheat, corn, and barley. As we travel higher, the air becomes chilly. The highest point of our trip is about 11,800 feet above sea level. The countryside looks bleak and barren, for there are no crops growing here. High above us rise great peaks that are always covered with ice and snow.

Because we are still in the tropics, temperatures here in the mountains do not change very much from month to month. However, there are great differences between temperatures in the sun and in the shade. When we stand in the bright sunlight, we feel very hot. A few feet away in the shade, we feel cool.

When we compare the relief map on page 12 with the temperature maps on page 18, we can locate the parts of South America in which the mountains and the highlands make the climate cooler. We can see that the only part of South America that has a cold climate is in the Andes Mountains.

**The climate is generally mild south of the tropics.** In the southern part of South America, as in other lands outside the tropics, there are changing seasons. However, when we look at the top map on page 18, we see that summers in the far southern part of South America are warm, rather than hot. The bottom map shows us that winter temperatures are cool, rather than cold, except in the high Andes Mountains. Even at the very southernmost tip of South America, winters are not so cold as in the parts of North America which are just as far away from the equator.

The shape of South America helps to cause the mild climate in the far south. Here the continent is very narrow. During the summer, the waters of the vast Pacific Ocean become warm much more slowly than the land. Therefore, the constant westerly winds that blow from the Pacific bring mild summer weather to the far south. In winter, the Pacific loses its heat more slowly than the land. West winds from the ocean bring mild winters to this part of South America. The lowest winter temperatures average between twenty and thirty degrees.

# Wet Lands

Receives 60 inches of
rain or more per year.

**Tropical lands where the rainfall is heavy.** About half of South America receives heavy rainfall. Most of these wet lands are in the tropical part of the continent. The rainfall map on page 22 shows the areas that receive sixty inches or more of rainfall each year. This is at least five feet of rain. In the western part of the Amazon Lowland, the yearly rainfall is more than one hundred inches.

West of the Andes Mountains, on parts of the Pacific coast of Colombia, the rainfall is about 280 inches a year.

The Amazon River and its tributaries* drain most of the vast area of heavy rainfall in tropical South America. In most of this land of heavy rainfall, there is some rain throughout the year. However, some months of the year are much wetter than others. In the far western part of the Amazon Lowland, where the yearly rainfall is over one hundred inches, the rainiest months are from November through March. In November, the waters at the western end of the Amazon begin to rise. In March and April, the southern tributaries empty

**A rainy day in Belém, Brazil.** Parts of the Amazon Lowland receive more than one hundred inches of rainfall each year. How do you think this heavy rainfall affects the Amazon River?

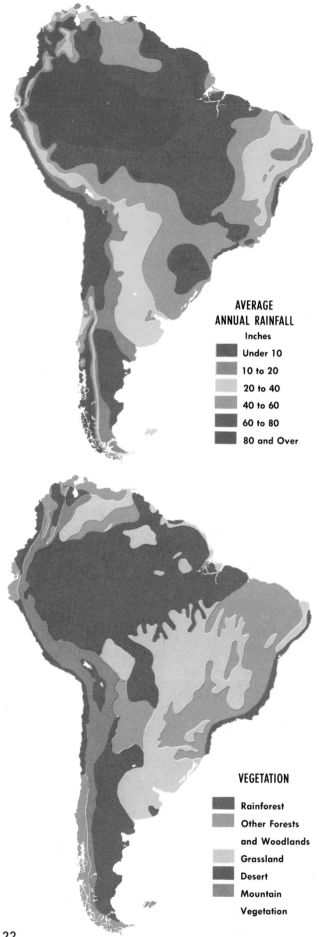

AVERAGE
ANNUAL RAINFALL
Inches
Under 10
10 to 20
20 to 40
40 to 60
60 to 80
80 and Over

VEGETATION
Rainforest
Other Forests
and Woodlands
Grassland
Desert
Mountain
Vegetation

their floodwaters into the main river. At this time the level of the Amazon sometimes rises as much as forty feet, flooding the land along the river. Until June, the Amazon continues to increase in volume. This great river carries more water to the sea than any other river in the world.

Let us compare the rainfall and vegetation maps on this page. We can see that parts of the wet lands of the tropics are covered by dense rainforest, and that other parts are grassland. The trees of the rainforest grow well where the climate is hot and moist throughout the year, as it is along the Amazon. In some parts of the wet lands of the tropics, however, there is a dry season in which little or no rain falls for several months. There is not enough moisture during the dry season for forests to grow, so tall grass and scattered trees cover these areas. When we compare the map on page 9 with the rainfall and vegetation maps on this page, we notice a large grassland area in Brazil. Although this area receives from sixty to eighty inches of rain each year, the dry season is so long that forests cannot grow.

**Lands south of the tropics that receive heavy rainfall.** One of the wettest areas in South America is in the southernmost part of the continent. (See rainfall map on this page.) Parts of this area receive more than two hundred inches of rainfall every year. Strong, moist winds from the Pacific blow across this part of South America all year round. These damp winds are forced to rise when they reach the Andes Mountains. As they rise and cool, they lose their moisture in the form of heavy rain or snow.

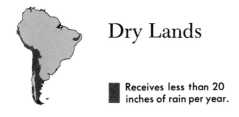

# Dry Lands

**Lands that receive little rainfall.** Only about one eighth of South America is very dry. These dry lands receive less than twenty inches of rainfall each year. One section of South America that receives little rain is in eastern Brazil. A few small areas along the northern coast of the continent are also very dry. As the rainfall map on page 22 shows, the largest area of dry lands in South America lies along much of the western coast and extends through the far southeastern part of the continent. Part of this dry area is a vast plateau called Pata-

gonia. Patagonia covers nearly all of southern Argentina and a small part of Chile. (Compare maps on pages 9 and 12.) As we learned earlier, winds from the Pacific lose their moisture when they reach the Andes. Therefore, after crossing the mountains, they are dry and bring little rain to Patagonia.

**South America's coastal desert.** Part of the dry area in the west is a desert that extends for about two thousand miles along the coasts of Peru and northern Chile. This desert receives less than two inches of rainfall per year. In some parts of the desert, rain has not fallen for many years. Wide, barren stretches of gravel and shifting sand dunes cover much of the land. In some places, the desert is made up of mountains. Only where the land is irrigated by streams that flow down from the

**Dry grazing lands in Patagonia.** The vast, dry plateau called Patagonia is located in the southern part of South America. Why does this part of the continent receive little rainfall each year?

high Andes Mountains is there enough moisture for crops to grow.

The winds that blow across this part of South America seldom bring rain. Before they reach the land, the winds from the Pacific blow over a cold ocean current that flows northward along the coast. These cool winds bring clouds and cool air to the desert, but very little rain. Winds from the east must cross the Andes Mountains before they reach the desert. These winds drop their moisture on the eastern slopes of the mountains. They bring no rain to the land on the western side.

## Lands of Moderate Rainfall

■ Receives 20 to 60 inches of rain per year.

About three eighths of South America receives a moderate amount of rain. Here the yearly rainfall is between twenty and sixty inches. Most of South America's best farming and grazing lands are in these areas of moderate rainfall. Let us compare the crop maps on pages 90 and 91 with the rainfall map on page 22. These maps show that most of South America's corn, wheat, coffee, and sugarcane are grown on farmlands that receive a moderate amount of rain. When we compare the cattle map on page 95 with the rainfall map, we see that most of South America's cattle are also raised in areas of moderate rainfall.

**Harvesting oats on a farm in Chile.** Most of South America's best farming and grazing lands are in areas that receive a moderate amount of rain.

## A Problem To Solve

In South America, there are many different climates. The weather in some areas is hot and rainy all year round. In other areas, the climate is too cool and dry for crops to grow. Why does climate differ from one part of South America to another? To solve this problem, you will need to make several hypotheses. (See pages 2-5 of the Skills Manual.) In forming your hypotheses, consider how each of the following affects climate in South America:

1. distance from the equator
2. land features
3. winds from the Pacific Ocean

## Exploring on Your Own

Violent earthquakes sometimes shake the land in the Andes Mountains. Do research about earthquakes, and then write a report that includes answers to the following questions.

1. What causes earthquakes?
2. In what parts of the world are earthquakes most common?
3. What are some of the effects of a major earthquake?
4. What are some of the most famous earthquakes that have occurred in the last hundred years? (You may wish to describe one of these earthquakes and tell about its effects.)

The suggestions on pages 13-18 of the Skills Manual will be helpful in finding information and writing an interesting report.

## Make Discoveries With Maps

The highland region of South America is made up of three parts: the Guiana Highlands, the Brazilian Highlands, and Patagonia. Locate these areas on the map on page 12. Then compare this map with other maps in this book to discover the following information:

1. the elevation of most of the land in the region
2. countries in which the highlands are located
3. rainfall received in various parts of the highlands
4. types of vegetation found in each of the highland areas

## Make a Relief Map of South America

South America is a large continent with many different land features. Make a relief map of this continent, using papier-mâché. First, you will need to trace an outline of the continent from a map in a large atlas. Use carbon paper to transfer this outline onto heavy cardboard. Then, form the continent out of papier-mâché. Using the map on page 12 as a guide, build up the highlands and the mountains out of more papier-mâché. Paint the land regions different colors. You may wish to show rivers, lakes, and the borders of the South American countries and territories. You may also wish to use thumbtacks to indicate the locations of some of South America's large cities.

## Discover More About Glaciers

The only part of South America that has a cold climate is in the Andes Mountains region. Some valleys high in the Andes are so cold that glaciers have formed in them. To discover more about these great rivers of ice, do research in other sources to find the following information:

1. kinds of glaciers found in the world
2. how glaciers are formed
3. how glaciers cause erosion

Then prepare an oral report describing what you have learned. You may wish to illustrate your report with pictures or drawings of glaciers.

## Use Your Imagination

Lake Titicaca is one of the largest lakes in South America. Imagine that you have been asked to write an article about this scenic lake for a travel magazine. Do research about the lake and the surrounding countryside before you begin to write. You may wish to include information about the following:

1. the location of Lake Titicaca
2. the lake's height above sea level
3. the types of boats used on the lake

Pages 15 and 113 of this book contain information that will be useful in writing your article. Refer to the suggestions on pages 13-15 of the Skills Manual for help in finding information in other sources.

# Part 2

# History and Government

As you do research about history and government in South America, you will be able to discover some of the many changes that have taken place on the continent during the past five centuries. The following questions will help guide you in your research.

- Why did the Europeans want to explore South America? In what ways did their coming affect the peoples who were living on the continent?
- How did the South American colonies eventually gain their independence?
- Did independence help to improve the people's way of life? Explain your answer.
- What kinds of government have been established in South America since independence?
- What are some of the problems that governments in South America face today?

**An Inca fortress at Cuzco, Peru.** In the 1500's, when the Spaniards first came to Peru, Cuzco was the capital city of the Inca Empire. What caused this empire to fall?

# 3   Early History

No one knows when the first people came to South America. Several thousand years ago, however, primitive Indians were living on this continent. Most of these people were hunters and fishermen. For weapons they used bows and arrows, sticks, and harpoons. In the western part of the continent, a great civilization gradually developed. The Indians of this civilization lived in the Inca Empire.

An Inca legend says that long ago the sun-god created two people—a man and a woman. The sun-god gave the Inca, or ruler, and his wife a golden staff and sent them forth to rule and teach the savage Indian tribes. They were to begin their work where the golden staff sank into the ground and disappeared. The Inca and his wife traveled across the mountains from Lake Titicaca. After a long journey, they found a beautiful valley. On a mountainside overlooking the valley, their golden staff vanished into the earth. Here the Inca and his wife founded the city of Cuzco. This city became the center of the Inca Empire. By the time the Spaniards came to South America, in the sixteenth century, the Inca Empire extended about three thousand miles along the western coast. (See map on page 33.)

If we travel in the mountains of Peru today, we can see why these people believed that the sun was their protector. Here on the "roof of the world," more than two miles above the level of the sea, the sun gives warmth and light during the day. When its last rays sink behind the snowcapped mountains, however, the air becomes bitterly cold. Only when the sun returns at dawn is there warmth again.

**The Inca Indians.** The people of the Inca Empire were strong and of medium height. The men usually wore a shirt-like garment covered with a poncho.* In extremely cold weather they also wore a cloak or a small blanket. In the mountains, where the weather was cold, clothing was usually made of llama* or alpaca* wool. Along the warm coastal lowlands of the empire, cotton was used for weaving most of the cloth. The Inca and his nobles wore clothing made of the silky fleece of the vicuña.*

If we had lived in the Inca Empire, we would have been members of one of three social classes. In the highest class were the Inca and his family. The next class was made up of nobles, which included the high state officials and their families. Most of the people were members of the third class, the class of the common people.

The Inca Indians did not live in a democracy. The common people had no political rights or privileges. There were no elections. Every part of their lives was controlled by their rulers.

Although the people had no real freedom, they did have security. Each family was given as much land as it needed to raise food. Extra food was stored so that there would be enough during times of emergency. The wise rulers tried to make their subjects happy and also prosperous.

*See Glossary

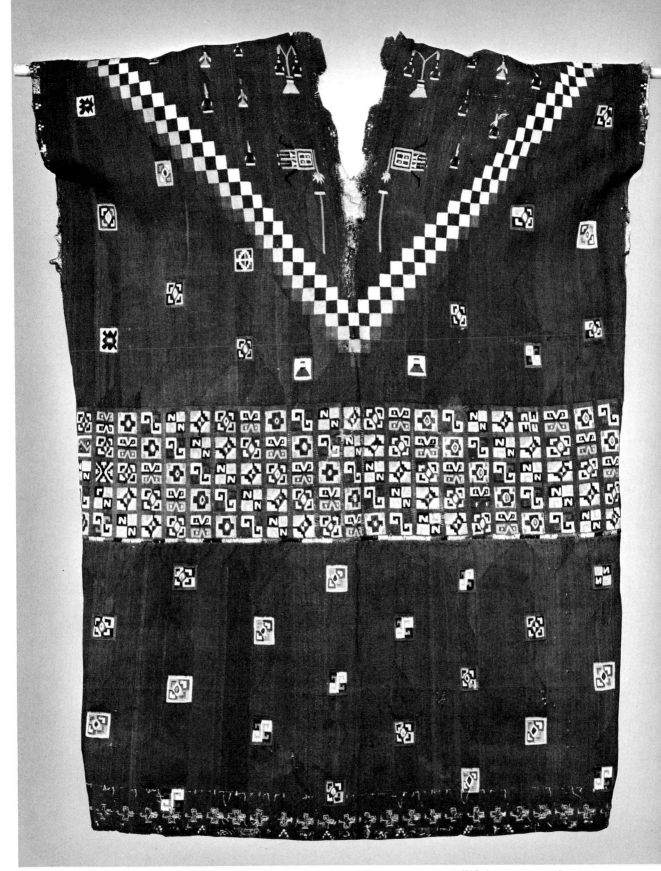

**A shirt made by an Inca Indian** hundreds of years ago. The Incas were skillful weavers. What materials did they use to make their clothing? Why do you suppose the clothing worn by the Inca and his nobles was made from a different material than the clothing worn by the common people?

Cooperation

See pages 130-134

**An Inca-style bridge** over a river in Peru. The Incas were skillful engineers. Bridges much like the ones they built are still used today in some parts of South America. Do you suppose the Incas could have built the excellent bridges, fortresses, and roads that they did if they hadn't cooperated with one another? Why do you think this? Do you suppose the Incas needed to cooperate with one another in order to build their great empire? Explain your answer.

**The skills of the Incas.** The Inca Indians were very skillful farmers. They cultivated the mountain valleys and the gentle slopes which surrounded them. On the steeper slopes, the farmers built terraces. These terraces were narrow shelves of land on the mountainsides. On these flat strips of land the Incas also planted crops. During the dry season, the farmland was irrigated with water from distant rivers and lakes. Along the dry coast, the Inca farmers built many canals and ditches. These canals and ditches carried water to the fields from streams which flowed down the mountainsides.

The Incas built excellent roads to connect the different parts of the empire. A stone road extended through the Andes from what is now Quito, Ecuador, southward through Cuzco and into the central part of what is now Chile. Another road, made of sun-baked clay, stretched along the coast from northern Peru to the central part of Chile. Each of these main highways was from fifteen to twenty-five feet wide. The road through the Andes was an engineering marvel. It ran over stony plateaus and snow-covered ridges. In some places it was more than sixteen thousand feet above the level of the sea.

The first suspension bridges of South America were built by Inca engineers. They wove thick, heavy cables from plant fibers. Then they stretched these cables across the gorge or river they wanted to cross. A flooring of sticks and matting was laid across the cables, and a handrail was added. These unusual hanging bridges swayed back and forth with the weight of those passing over them. Such bridges are still being used today by Indians in some places in the mountains.

Some of the Inca fortresses look as if they had been built by a race of giants. One of the massive granite blocks in the fortress near Cuzco is twenty-seven feet high, fourteen feet wide, and twelve feet thick. The Incas fitted these huge boulders together so carefully that even today it is impossible to insert a knife blade between many of them.

Francisco **Pizarro** and a small army captured and later killed the ruler of the Inca Indians at Cajamarca. The common people of the Inca Empire were helpless without their ruler. Why was this so?

**Pizarro comes to Peru.** Early in the 1500's, Spanish explorers began hearing rumors of the rich empire of the Incas. One of the men who was most excited by these stories of wealth was Francisco Pizarro. In January of 1531, Pizarro and his men left Panama and sailed southward until strong winds forced them to land on the coast of what is now Ecuador. (See maps on pages 9 and 33.) From here they continued their journey southward by land. Some of the men rode horses, which the Indians had never seen before. Although some of the Indians they met were friendly, others attacked the Spaniards. After many months, Pizarro and his small army reached the foothills of the snowcapped Andes. Day after day, they climbed upward into the mountains. Finally they came to the Inca city of Cajamarca, high in the Andes.

When Pizarro and his men entered Cajamarca, the city was strangely empty. Not a single human being or animal could be found in the deserted streets. On the nearby mountainsides, however, were the Inca and his army. During the afternoon, Pizarro sent a message to the Inca, inviting him to the city for a friendly visit. The Inca agreed to come the next day. All night long Pizarro and his men watched as the Indians' campfires gleamed on the surrounding mountains. At last the Inca entered the city with a group of nobles and some of his army.

All were unarmed. Without warning, the Spaniards attacked the defenseless Indians. The Inca was captured and thousands of his people were killed.

As ransom for his freedom, the Inca offered one room filled with gold and another room filled twice with silver. As more and more gold and silver arrived, the Spaniards were amazed at the Inca's wealth. When the rooms had been filled, the greedy soldiers melted all the rare objects of Inca art into bars of gold and silver. Finally they murdered the Inca. The common people of the empire, who had never had to think or act for themselves, were helpless without their ruler. The Inca Empire had fallen.

**Other Spanish conquerors.** The conquerors were not content with the gold and silver of Peru. They were excited by the idea that there might be other rich empires in South America. In 1540, Gonzalo Pizarro, a half brother of the conqueror of Peru, traveled eastward from the city of Quito, in the Andes. He hoped to find vast forests of valuable spice trees in a region called the Land of Cinnamon. The explorers descended the eastern slopes of the rugged mountains. Then they pushed their way through forests of gigantic trees. On and on they went, cutting through the dense underbrush. Their food rotted and spoiled in the damp, hot climate. Many of the men died. At last, the starving, exhausted men reached a swift river. Here they built a crude boat so that some of them could go down the river to search for food.

Half of the men, led by Francisco de Orellana, floated down the river in the boat. These men never returned to their starving comrades. Instead they drifted from one river into another. Finally they floated into a river that was wider than any they had seen in South America. They had reached the Amazon River. These explorers followed the great Amazon River all the way to the Atlantic Ocean. They had crossed almost the entire continent of South America. (See map below.)

In 1540, Francisco Pizarro sent Pedro de Valdivia into what is now Chile to establish Spanish settlements. Valdivia and his men found the warlike Araucanian Indians living there. These Indians were not as easy to conquer as

**Spanish explorers** traveled through many parts of South America during the 1500's. What did Francisco de Orellana discover during his journey?

HISTORY

Inca Empire at its Greatest Extent

Francisco Pizarro, 1531-1533

Francisco de Orellana, 1540-1541

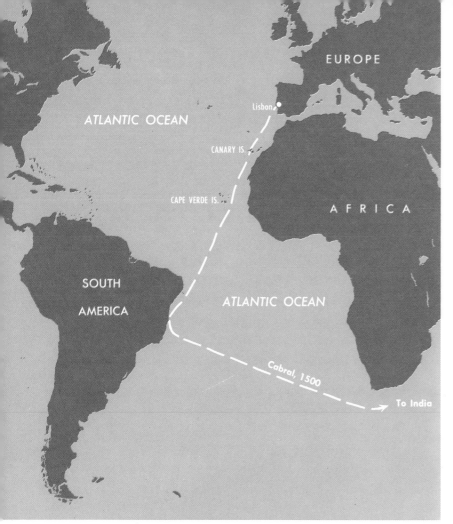

The Portuguese began coming to the New World in the early 1500's. The map above shows the route of Cabral, who landed in South America and claimed for Portugal the land now called Brazil.

the Incas had been. There was bitter warfare between the Araucanian forces and the Spaniards.

The Spaniards also found hostile Indians in other parts of South America. In 1516, the explorer Juan Díaz de Solís sailed into the great Río de la Plata. When he went ashore, however, he and most of his men were killed by the Indians. In 1536, Pedro de Mendoza built a fort where the city of Buenos Aires now stands. However, hostile Indians drove the people from the fort. The Spaniards did not start a settlement at Buenos Aires again until 1580.

**Portugal in the New World.** In 1500, Pedro Alvares Cabral, a Portuguese navigator, sailed into a harbor along the eastern coast of South America. He planted a cross on the coast and claimed the land for the king of Portugal. This land is now called Brazil. For many years after Cabral's discovery, Portugal paid little attention to Brazil. Finally, the Portuguese king became worried because Spanish and French traders were sailing to Portugal's territory in the New World. The king also heard stories of the great riches found by the Spaniards in South America. He decided to divide Brazil among thirteen wealthy Portuguese who were to establish settlements and develop the colony. The first official settlement was founded at São Vicente in 1532. Other settlements were soon established. In 1549, the king

Tomé de Sousa became the first governor-general of the Portuguese colony of Brazil. Why did the Portuguese king become eager to have settlements established in Portugal's territory in the New World?

appointed Tomé de Sousa the first governor-general of Brazil.

The early settlers in Brazil did not find any great treasures of silver and gold which they could send back to Portugal. However, they did begin to grow a valuable crop. This was sugarcane, which they brought to South America from the Madeira Islands.* Sugarcane grew very well along the northeastern coast of Brazil. Huge fields of this crop were also planted farther south. The settlers sent valuable cargoes of sugar back to Portugal. During the seventeenth century, Brazil was one of the world's most important sources of sugar.

The Portuguese also continued their search for gold and silver. From the

small settlements along the coast, bold adventurers marched inland through mile after mile of forest. They traveled far up the rivers. In 1698, gold was discovered in the central part of what is now the state of Minas Gerais, Brazil. Later, diamonds were found north of the goldfields.

The discovery of gold and diamonds brought a great number of people to Brazil. Towns quickly grew up in the wilderness near the newly discovered mines. For about a hundred years, thousands of people lived and worked here. After the rush for gold and diamonds, many people left the mining regions. Some remained, however, to farm the fertile land and to raise cattle.

# 4  Later History

**A Problem To Solve**

In the early 1800's, people living in the Spanish colonies in South America revolted and fought to gain their independence. Why did the colonists revolt against Spanish rule? In order to solve this problem, you will need to make several hypotheses. In forming your hypotheses, you will need to consider how the following helped to bring about revolution:

1. the way the colonies were governed
2. Spanish trade restrictions
3. events taking place in other parts of the world

See Skills Manual, pages 2-5

**Life in the colonies.** For a few of the families living in the colonies of South America, life was very carefree and exciting. Although the colonies were far away from Spain and Portugal, these wealthy families tried to live just as they would have lived in Europe. Life was a pleasant round of parties and festivals. Each afternoon the ladies rode through the bumpy streets in richly decorated carriages. Their homes were furnished with expensive carpets and fine furniture from Europe.

For most of the people, however, life in the colonies was very different. Many people of mixed European and Indian blood, called mestizos, worked on small farms or earned their living as unskilled laborers. Indians were forced to work in the mines or on the huge estates of the wealthy families. There were no festive parties for these people.

**Discontent in the Spanish colonies.** As the years passed, many of the wealthy people living in the Spanish colonies became dissatisfied with the strict control under which they lived. Spain did not allow the colonists to choose their own officials. All the officials were appointed by the king. People born in

**A plaza in Lima, Peru, during colonial times.** Life in the South American colonies was pleasant for a few wealthy families, who were able to live much as they would have lived in Europe.

South America were seldom appointed as officials, even if their parents had come from Spain. The Spanish colonists were also forbidden to trade with any other country but Spain. All the goods which they needed had to be bought from Spain. In return, each colony had to send its raw materials to Spain, for the colonies were not even allowed to trade with each other. Those who mined

gold or silver were not allowed to keep all this wealth for themselves. One fifth of everything mined in the Spanish colonies had to be sent to Spain for the king. This was a large amount to send to a king so far away.

As the eighteenth century came to a close, people in the colonies began to think more and more about independence. They heard of the Declaration of Independence in the colonies of North America. News also came from Europe of the revolution in France. When the Spanish colonists saw that freedom and independence were being won in other parts of the world, they wondered if they, too, could win their freedom. In 1808, Napoleon, the emperor of France, conquered Spain and made his brother Joseph the king of Spain. Now the ruler of the colonies was not even Spanish. This was the time to revolt.

**The leaders of the revolution.** Although many of the colonists were dissatisfied with Spanish rule, not all of them wanted independence. Many of the people who had been born in Spain did not want to change the governments of the colonies. They wanted to keep the Spanish in control. Some of the people felt that they should be allowed to choose their own government officials, but they wanted to remain loyal to Spain. Others were ready to fight for independence at once. To gain their independence, the colonists needed men to lead them.

Loyalty

See pages 130-134

**San Martín leading his men** through a pass in the Andes Mountains. San Martín was a brilliant soldier who used his military training and experience to help the people of the South American colonies gain their independence. The men who fought with San Martín suffered many hardships. Yet, they wanted very much to be free from Spanish rule. Do you think these men were disloyal to Spain? Give reasons for your answer. Do you think these men showed any loyalty at all? Explain your answer.

Throughout the colonies, men of ability and courage rose to unite and guide their people. Each of these men was important in helping the colonists, but there were two men who were more important than all the others. They were José de San Martín and Simón Bolívar.

**San Martín leads the southern Spanish colonies.** José de San Martín was the son of a wealthy Spanish family that lived

in Argentina for a number of years. When San Martín was very young, his family moved back to Spain. There, he grew up to become an officer in the Spanish army. He never forgot the land of his birth, however. He often talked with people who came to Europe from the colonies. When he learned that the South American people wanted their independence, San Martín offered to use his military training and experience to help them gain their freedom. In 1812, he returned to South America to train a small army in Argentina.

San Martín knew that Peru was the stronghold of the Spanish army in South America. Before all of South America could be free, the Spaniards would have to be driven out of Peru. San Martín decided upon a dangerous plan. He would march from his native Argentina across the Andes Mountains into Chile.

When he had freed Chile, he would then go by sea to attack Peru.

Aided by a Chilean officer named Bernardo O' Higgins, San Martín gathered an army of about four thousand Argentines and Chileans. In January, 1817, the well-trained army left Mendoza, Argentina. For twenty-one days the men marched across the rugged Andes. During the day the sun was bright and hot, but at night the air was bitterly cold. In places the trail was so narrow that the men had to go in single file. Finally, after many hardships, the army reached the valley of central Chile. The Spaniards were taken by surprise and were quickly defeated. Then the victorious army marched into Santiago, the capital of Chile. O'Higgins was given charge of the Chilean government. In 1818 the entire colony of Chile was declared independent from Spain.

Now San Martín began trying to get ships and men to sail to Peru. Finally in August, 1820, everything was ready. San Martín and his men sailed northward along the western coast of South America.

After they arrived in Peru, San Martín and his men talked to the people about independence. He told them that he had come to help them gain their independence from Spain. For months, San Martín and his army camped outside the city of Lima, while the fleet blocked the nearby harbor at Callao. Gradually, more and more of the colonists joined together for independence. Even whole companies of Spanish soldiers deserted and joined San Martín's army. In July, 1821, the Spanish governor fled with his remaining troops to the mountains of the interior. San Martín had won the city of Lima.

**Bolívar leads the fight for independence in the north.** While San Martín was working in the southern part of South America, other men had been struggling for independence in the Spanish colonies to the north. Simón Bolívar was the leader of these men. As a young man he had vowed that he would devote his life to freeing South America from Spanish control.

By the middle of 1822, Bolívar had freed the Spanish colonies in the north, and Peru was the only colony in South America still held by the Spaniards.

**Bolívar and his men** helped people in what are now the countries of Colombia, Ecuador, Peru, Venezuela, and Bolivia gain their independence from Spain. Bolívar became the first president of Colombia.

Although San Martín had freed the cities of Lima and Callao, the Spanish army still held the rest of Peru. Something had to be done to free all of the colony. On July 25, 1822, Bolívar and San Martín met at the town of Guayaquil, in what is now Ecuador. San Martín wanted to work with Bolívar to free Peru. However, the two men could not agree, so San Martín decided to return to Argentina. Bolívar and his men continued to fight against the Spaniards in Peru. In 1826, the last Spanish soldiers surrendered, and Spain no longer con-

trolled any of the South American colonies.

**Portuguese settlers in Brazil gain their independence.** While the people of the Spanish colonies in South America were fighting for their independence, the people of Brazil were still being ruled by Portugal. Brazil even became the center of government for the Portuguese Empire.

In 1807, Emperor Napoleon sent French troops into Portugal. Before the soldiers reached the capital, the Portuguese prince João and the royal family escaped and sailed for Brazil, their colony in South America. They set up their court in Rio de Janeiro. Brazil prospered under João's rule.

Then in 1821, João returned to Portugal. He left his son Dom Pedro to rule Brazil. At this time, many people in Brazil believed that their country should be independent from Portugal. However, Brazil was soon to be treated as a colony again. Dom Pedro was even ordered to return to Portugal. He refused, and on September 7, 1822, he declared Brazil's independence. He was crowned emperor of Brazil.

Dom Pedro II became emperor after his father. He ruled the country wisely and well for almost fifty years. When the people talked of making Brazil a republic, he did not interfere. Brazil finally became a republic on November 15, 1889. By his wise and strong rule, Dom Pedro II had given his country time to grow and progress.

**Years of unrest.** For many years after the colonies in South America became independent, there was much unrest among the people. This early period of independence is often called the Age of Dictators. In many new countries, the government officials were not chosen by free elections. Instead, army officials often fought among themselves for government offices. Since most of the people had no experience in governing themselves, these military men often gained control. In fact, throughout most of the nineteenth century, dictators ruled in every Spanish South American country.

A painting called *Independence or Death* shows Dom Pedro as he declared Brazil's independence from Portugal. Dom Pedro was then crowned emperor of Brazil. When did Brazil become a republic?

# 5 Government

**Rules
and
Government**

See pages 130-134

**A political rally in Chile.** After gaining independence from European rule, many South American countries had great difficulty in establishing stable governments. For example, Chile has had at least three different types of government since gaining its independence from Spain in 1818. Ecuador had twelve different presidents during one nine-year period in recent history. Discuss the following question as a class. Is it important for a country to have a stable government? To prepare for your discussion, the class might divide into committees. Each committee should choose a different South American country and then do research in other sources about the history of that country's government.

A machine shop in Bogotá, Colombia. During the past ten years, Colombia has made much economic progress. How do you suppose the development of new industries helps a nation's standard* of living?

**Democratic governments have been established in some South American countries.** In recent years, the people in some countries in South America have been able to free themselves from the rule of their military dictators. (See page 42.) South Americans in Colombia, Chile, Venezuela, and Uruguay are now able to choose their own government officials in free elections.

One South American country that now has a well-established democratic government is Colombia. The Colombian constitution guarantees many freedoms, such as freedom of religion and freedom of speech, to all Colombians. A new president is elected by the people every four years.

During the past ten years, the Colombian government has made much progress in solving many of the serious problems faced by most South American countries. (See pages 45-48.) Colombia's production of goods and services is now increasing at about 6 percent per year. More Colombian children and adults are now receiving an education than ever before. Land reforms have made it possible for many tenant farmers to obtain their own farmland.

**Dictators continue to rule much of South America.** In many other countries in South America, powerful dictators or men chosen by the military leaders continue to control the governments. In these dictatorships, the people do not have free elections. They do not have freedom of speech or freedom of the press, and people who criticize the government are sometimes arrested and sent to jail without being tried in court.

Most dictators claim they want power only in order to improve their country-

*See Glossary

44

men's way of life. Because these dictators are often supported by wealthy landowners, however, their rule does more to aid the rich than to improve the lives of the poor people.

**Governments in South America face serious problems.** In most South American countries, the governments must help provide a better way of life for the people. In order to do this, however, they must solve a number of serious problems. Many South Americans do not have enough food, adequate shelter, or good jobs. They also need better schools and more nurses and doctors.

There are several reasons why these problems exist. Most of the people in South America still earn their living by farming. Much of the best farmland on the continent is owned by a small number of wealthy people. The farmers who work on these huge estates often cannot afford proper food, housing, or medical care for their families. Many farmers who have land of their own do not live any better. Their farms are usually only a few acres in area, and are often located in places where the land is rugged or the soil is poor for growing crops. Also, these farmers do not use modern machinery or scientific farming methods. As a result, they produce barely enough food to keep themselves alive.

In recent years, many people have left the rural areas of South America and moved to the cities in search of a better life. However, most of them lack the skills needed for getting jobs in modern industry. Also, there are not enough jobs in factories, stores, and offices to provide employment for all the people who want to work. Large numbers of these people cannot find employment or must work at jobs that

**A South American doctor and nurse** attending a patient. Providing better health care is one of the problems most South American governments must solve. What other problems do they face?

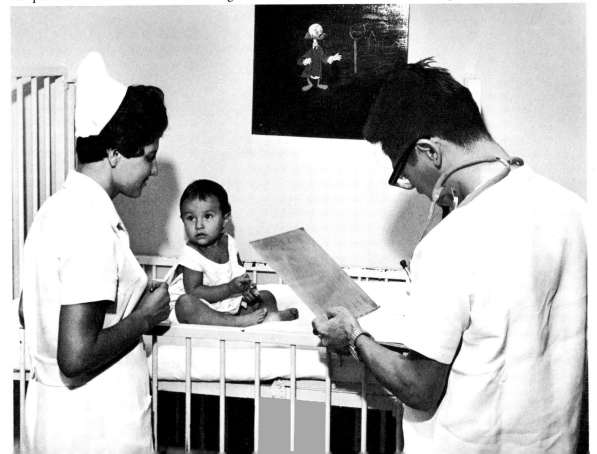

**Farming** is still the way most people in South America earn their living. Life is very difficult for most of these farmers and their families. What facts help to explain why this is so?

pay very low wages. They have to live in dirty, overcrowded slums without electricity or running water.

Disease is a serious problem in South America. Disease germs are often spread by insects or by impure water supplies. Many people cannot obtain the variety of foods needed for good health. In most South American countries, there are not enough hospitals or doctors to take care of all those who are sick. It is not surprising that many children die before they reach school age.

With more education, the less fortunate people of South America might be better able to solve some of their pressing problems. However, about one third of the people in South America cannot read or write. There are not enough schools for all the children to attend.

escape from poverty is also increasing rapidly. This makes it extremely difficult to achieve progress toward raising the standard of living.

**A continent of rising expectations.** Many people in South America are becoming increasingly dissatisfied because life is so difficult for them. They are beginning to demand a greater share of the good things that most people in Western industrialized nations have. For many years, most people in South America took their poverty for granted because they did not know that there was any other way to live. Travel, trade, and communications have increased so much in recent years, however, that this is no longer true. In movies and magazines, many South Americans see pictures of cars, washing machines, and other products commonly used by people in their own large cities and by people living in other countries, such as the United States. What they see is making them realize that some people in the world have a much easier, more comfortable way of life than they do. They want this way of life for themselves. Because South America's people are beginning to expect more, we say that they are going through a "revolution of rising expectations."

Their rising expectations are making South American people restless. Often they rebel against their governments, seeking the reforms that they hope will make their lives more comfortable. Sometimes these people succeed in overthrowing their governments. When this happens, they expect their new governments to provide factories, schools, hospitals, and other institutions needed to bring about the better way of life they want. When the new governments

Also, there is a shortage of well-trained teachers. Lack of education is one of the main obstacles to raising the standard* of living for the people of South America.

All of these problems are made more serious by the fact that the population of the South American continent is growing rapidly each year. Therefore, the number of people who need help to are unable to provide these things immediately, the people are disappointed. They become even more dissatisfied and restless. Often they will turn again to rebellion or revolution as a solution to their problems. As a result of this, few South American countries have been able to develop stable governments. Frequently, a president or a dictator will not be able to keep himself and his government officials in power for more than a year or two. Some governments rule for an even shorter period of time. During 1970, for example, Bolivia had four new governments in the space of three days. Without reliable, stable governments, the people of South America find it very difficult even to begin solving their problems.

**South Americans are working to achieve a better way of life.** During the past few years, some changes have taken place in South America. With help from the United States and with the aid of such world organizations as the United Nations and the World Bank, some South American governments have begun to provide their people with more schools, hospitals, and roads. Public health programs are helping to wipe out diseases that formerly killed thousands of people every year. Low-cost apartments are being built for large numbers of needy families.

Most South American countries are also making progress in improving agriculture and developing new industries. New farm machines and better agricultural methods are helping to raise crop production. Today, industry is growing rapidly throughout South America. New factories are supplying many products that South Americans formerly had to buy from other countries.

**In the auto-mechanics shop** of a school in Brazil. United Nations scholarships have made it possible for some South Americans to attend school and learn the skills needed to hold jobs in industry.

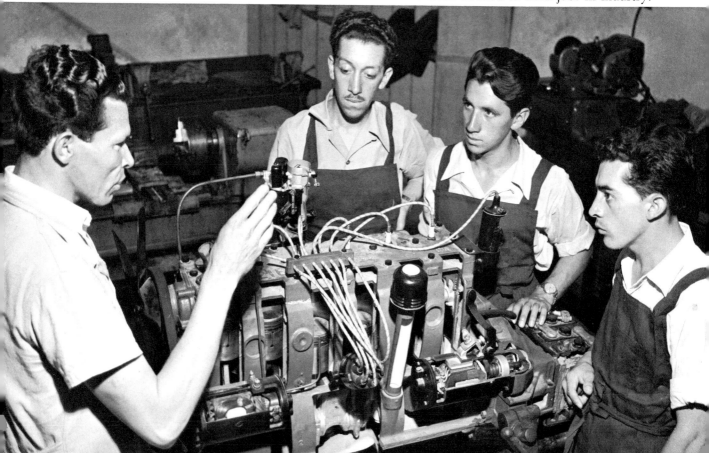

## Explore the Inca Civilization

Hundreds of years ago, the Inca Indians of South America developed a great civilization. They built an empire that extended about three thousand miles along the western coast of South America. As a class, make a study of this great civilization. First, the class should be divided into committees. Then each committee should select one or more of the following topics for special study. There may also be additional topics you would like to explore.

1. farming
2. government
3. arts and crafts
4. cities
5. record keeping
6. religion
7. architecture
8. transportation
9. language
10. education
11. social classes and ways of living (including information about the ways in which the people in each class met their physical needs)

The members of each committee should make a plan for doing research and decide how they will present the understandings they gain. In addition to preparing oral or written reports, consider presenting information in ways such as the following:

1. murals (such as a mural showing life in a city)
2. skits (such as a short play illustrating the daily life of a farmer and his family)
3. drawings and diagrams (such as a drawing of an Inca city or fortress)
4. models and dioramas (such as a model of a terraced mountain slope or of a hanging bridge)

The suggestions on pages 13-15 of the Skills Manual will help you to find the information you need to work together successfully in your committees.

## Use Your Imagination

After Columbus discovered the New World, Spanish and Portuguese explorers began coming to South America. Imagine that you were with Francisco de Orellana and his men during their exploration of the Amazon River. Write a letter to a friend telling about your exciting trip. In your letter, you may want to include information about the following:

1. what you had hoped to find on your journey
2. the land features and climate of the area through which you traveled
3. interesting plants and animals that you saw along the way
4. the actual results of the expedition

You may wish to do research in other sources before you begin to write. Refer to pages 13-15 of the Skills Manual for suggestions on finding information.

## Be a Biographer

In the early 1800's, all of the Spanish and Portuguese colonies in South America gained their independence. Listed below are three men who played important roles in helping the colonies to gain their independence.

José de San Martín
Simón Bolívar
Dom Pedro

Do research about one of these men and then write a short biography about him. Read your biography to the class and be prepared to answer any questions your classmates may ask.

## Keep Up With Current Events

Newspapers and magazines often contain articles about the countries of South America. With your classmates, make a bulletin-board display of articles you find that are especially interesting and informative. Include pictures in your display if possible. As a class, discuss and evaluate the information presented in each article. Keep in mind the suggestions for evaluating information on pages 15-17 of the Skills Manual.

## Make Discoveries About the United Nations

Many of the problems faced by the people of South America are shared by people all over the world. The United Nations, a worldwide organization, has established many agencies to help governments in South America and other parts of the world solve these serious problems. Do research in other sources to discover what some of these United Nations agencies are and how they are helping people all over the world. Then write a report summarizing your discoveries.

# Part 3

# People and Their Way of Life

As you do research in Part 3, you will discover that many different groups of people have made their homes in South America. How does life in South America today reflect the influence of these different groups of people? To answer this question, you will need to consider facts about the following:

- languages spoken in South America
- religions followed by the people
- arts and crafts of South America
- festivals held here
- sports enjoyed by South Americans

**Social Needs**

See pages 135-136

The two boys shown in the picture at left seem to be very curious about the flowers being sold by vendors in Rio de Janeiro. Imagine that you are one of these boys. Would you like to know more about these flowers and the men who are selling them? What questions would you like to have these men answer for you? Do you think it is important to make discoveries and learn new facts about people and things in the world around you? Give reasons for your answer.

# 6 People

**South America is a land of many peoples.** Many different groups of people live on the vast continent of South America. They do not all speak the same language or follow the same customs. Deep in the rainforests and high in the Andes Mountains live several million Indians whose ancestors came to South America centuries ago. Portuguese and Spanish people live in many of the cities throughout the continent. In the hot, wet lowlands along the tropical coasts are Negroes whose ancestors were brought from Africa as slaves during colonial times. Many people of these different groups have intermarried.* As a result, millions of people of mixed ancestry live in South America today.

*See Glossary

**The Spanish and Portuguese South Americans.** Many people living in South America today are descendants of the Spanish or the Portuguese. Most of these people have black hair, dark-brown eyes, and dark complexions. Often they live in fine homes that were built in the Spanish or Portuguese cities during the colonial days. Sometimes they own estates given to their families hundreds of years ago. Usually they are well educated.

South Americans of Spanish descent. Many people living in South America today are of Spanish or Portuguese descent. Why is this so?

Language

See pages 130-134

Many different groups of people live in South America. Not only do they follow different customs, but they also speak a wide variety of languages. In what ways do you suppose this great number of languages might affect communication among South America's people? Discuss this question as a class.

53

As we meet and speak with Spanish and Portuguese South Americans, we find that they still follow many of the traditions that the first settlers brought with them to South America long ago. Family life is very important. All the members of the family enjoy doing things together. Grandfathers and grandmothers, aunts and uncles, first cousins and second cousins see each other as often as possible. Sometimes the whole family group lives together in one large house.

The settlers who first came to South America left other traditions as well. They thought that working with their hands was very undignified. Sports and physical exercise were frowned upon. Even today, some South Americans do not like to work in their yards or to carry packages through the streets. They feel that servants should do this kind of work.

The early European settlers in South America also gave their languages to the peoples of today. In most of the towns in Brazil, Portuguese is spoken. Because Spanish explorers conquered other parts of South America, Spanish is the official language throughout most of the rest of the continent. However, many Indian languages are still spoken in South America, especially in areas that are located far away from the cities.

Almost everyone in South America follows the religion of the early conquerors. Roman Catholic cathedrals, churches, and monasteries are found in every country. When we visit small towns and big cities, we often hear the clanging of church bells.

**Indians of the mountains.** Today, about fourteen million Indians live in South America. They are descendants of the thousands of Indians who were living on this continent long before the Spanish and Portuguese began to settle here. Many of these Indian people live high in the Andes Mountains.

Most of the mountain Indians live and work much as their ancestors did hundreds of years ago. Instead of living in cities, they live in small villages. Usually these people are farmers or herders. In some places they farm on terraces built by their ancestors long ago. (See page 31 .)

The mountain Indians even wear the same kinds of clothing worn by their ancestors. In villages high in the mountains, it is usually so cold that the women wear half a dozen full skirts, one on top of another. As we walk through one of these Indian villages, we see women wearing skirts of bright orange, red, pink, blue, green, and purple. Usually they do not wear two

Physical
Needs

See pages 135-136

**Indian women and children at a Bolivian market.** Many mountain Indian women in South America wear several layers of brightly colored full skirts. These layers of material help to protect the women from the cold mountain air. In what other ways do mountain Indians in South America meet their physical needs? What type of shelter do they have? In what ways do they obtain the food they need?

skirts of the same color next to each other. Instead of coats, most of the women are wearing warm woolen blouses and heavy shawls. Everywhere we go, we see women wearing derby-shaped hats made of felt. They seem to like these hats so much that they wear them almost all the time.

The men of the village are dressed in homemade shirts and knee-length trousers. The ponchos over their shoulders are bright red with beautiful designs woven into the material. Some of the men also have warm woolen caps with long ear flaps.

Life in the Indian villages is very different from life in the cities. The homes are small huts made of stone or mud. Usually there are no stoves to heat these houses. During the day the people stay outdoors in the warm sunshine. At night they come inside to get out of the cold night air.

Many of the mountain Indians know little about the world outside their villages. They live from day to day, making a living as best they can from their land. However, these people do not wish to change their way of life. They do not want to leave their land for better fields in the lowlands. They prefer to stay here in the mountains, in the land of their ancestors. Most of these people still speak Indian languages that were spoken long ago.

**Indians of the lowlands.** In the hot, tropical lowlands of South America, many groups of primitive people live much as men did long before the coming of civilization. These are the primitive Indians of the Amazon Lowland and tropical lowlands in Colombia, Guyana, Surinam, and French Guiana. (See maps

POPULATION PER SQUARE MILE

- 0 to 10
- 10 to 75
- 75 to 250
- 250 to 500
- 500 and Over

**Population per square mile.** Why do you think so much of South America is thinly populated?

on pages 9 and 12.) Many of these Indians make their living as their ancestors did. They hunt animals and gather wild fruits and wild rice. They raise pigs, chickens, and some vegetables. Most of these people wear few clothes because the weather is hot and humid. Families live in simple one-room huts.

One such primitive tribe is the Jivaro people who live in eastern Ecuador. They are a proud and generous people who have kept many of their customs. They treat other people as equals so long as they do not break any of the

Indians of the Amazon Lowland. Many groups of primitive people make their homes in the tropical lowlands of South America. Why do we call these people "primitive"? How do they make their living?

strict tribal laws. The Jivaro people can be very cruel when angry. They are famous hunters who use blowguns with poisoned darts. They used to shrink the heads of enemies they had killed, but this practice is no longer allowed.

**Mestizos.** In South America, about one third of the people are of mixed ancestry. Most of these people are mestizos. They have both Indian and European ancestors. Mestizos usually have straight black hair and dark-brown eyes.

Many mestizos live in South America's cities. Some of these people are quite prosperous. Often they send their children to costly private schools. Some mestizos have their own businesses. Others work for the government. Still others are skilled laborers in South America's industries.

Many of South America's mestizos are very poor. They live in ugly, run-down buildings in the slum areas of the cities. Often they do not have enough to eat. They are not able to send their children to school. Trying to improve the lives of these people is one of South America's biggest problems.

**Negroes in Salvador, Brazil.** There are several million Negroes living in South America today. Their ancestors were brought to South America from the continent of Africa as slaves during colonial times.

**Negroes.** During colonial times, many Negroes were brought to South America from Africa to work on the plantations of the Spanish and Portuguese landowners. These landowners knew that African Negroes were used to the hot sunlight of the tropics and would be good workers. Today several million descendants of these people live in parts of South America where their ancestors were once slaves. Because of intermarriage, some of these Negroes are actually mixtures of several different peoples.

We can meet many people of African descent when we visit the city of Salvador, on the coast of Brazil. (See map on page 61.) Early in the morning we see many Negro women in the marketplace of the city. Some of these women are carrying large baskets on their heads as they walk through the streets selling their wares. The costumes of these gay, friendly women are a combination of African and European styles. Usually the women have turbans wrapped around their heads and brightly colored shawls draped over their shoulders. Their printed skirts are long and full. Often their shoes have wooden soles. Huge, heavy earrings and long, dangling beads complete their costumes.

**Other peoples.** During the last hundred years, many other peoples have come to South America. Often they have moved into lonely and unsettled regions. On the cool and windswept plateau of Patagonia, we find shepherds whose ancestors came from England, Scotland, or Wales. There are many Japanese people living near the city of São Paulo, Brazil. Large numbers of Germans have settled in southern Chile and southern Brazil. Their settlements often seem like small sections of Germany in South America. Some of the German people in southern Brazil still speak the German language. Many of their homes also remind us of Germany.

Not all the people who have come to South America have settled in particular cities or countries, however. There are thousands of Italian people living throughout South America. Wandering Syrian* merchants travel about in the interior of the continent. These men go from village to village, buying, selling, and trading.

After World War II, people from many European countries came to South America to find new homes. Today these newcomers from Austria, Switzerland, Greece, and many other lands are living near people whose ancestors came to South America hundreds of years ago.

**Italian women** at work on a coffee plantation near São Paulo, Brazil. Thousands of Italian people have made their homes in South America. After World War II, many Europeans came to this continent.

**Buenos Aires**, the capital of Argentina, is located on the southeastern coast of South America. This industrial city is the main seaport for Argentina's richest agricultural region, the Pampa.

# 7 Cities

We could travel for thousands of miles in South America and never see a city. Large sections of the interior of this continent are almost uninhabited. There are, however, important cities in South America. Let us visit some of these cities.

**Buenos Aires.** We are now flying over Río de la Plata* toward Buenos Aires, the capital of Argentina. (See map on opposite page.) About three and one-half million people live in this city on the southeastern coast of South America.

*See Glossary

Not far from the waterfront of the city, we see the famous *Casa Rosada*, or "Pink House." Here the president of Argentina and other officials of the government have their offices. A wide avenue leads westward from the *Casa Rosada* to the domed congress building. Nearby we see lovely parks.

Soon after our plane lands at Buenos Aires, we visit the busy waterfront. We see many riverboats which bring agricultural products down the Paraná

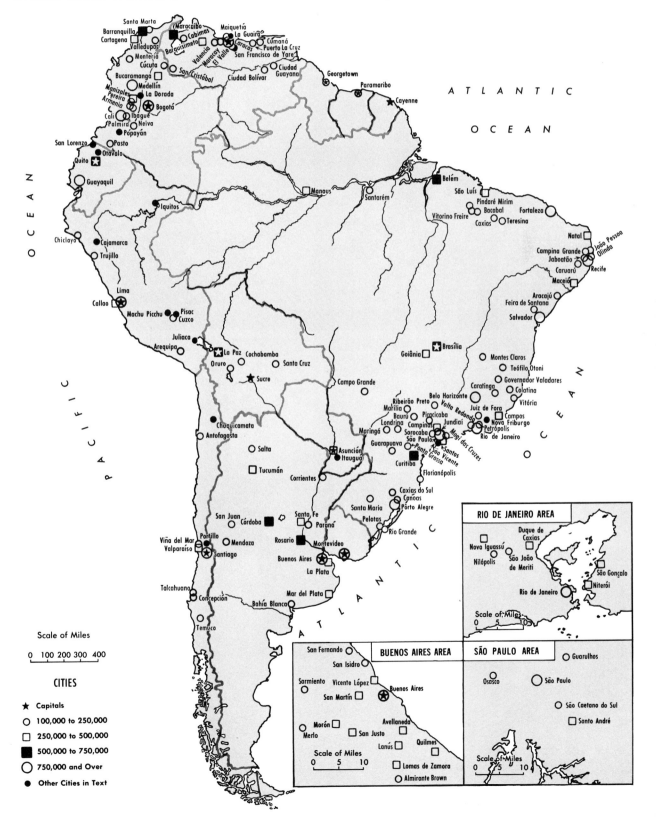

Scale of Miles

0 100 200 300 400

**CITIES**

★ Capitals
○ 100,000 to 250,000
□ 250,000 to 500,000
■ 500,000 to 750,000
◯ 750,000 and Over
● Other Cities in Text

River to the coast. Ships from many different countries are anchored alongside the docks. We see men loading cargoes of beef, wheat, and other agricultural products. Buenos Aires is the main port for Argentina's richest agricultural region, the Pampa.

Buenos Aires is also an industrial city. People in Buenos Aires work in food-processing plants, oil refineries, printing plants, and metalworks. Others have jobs making tires, automobiles, or chemicals.

Later in the day, we stroll along a wide, tree-shaded avenue that leads through the center of the city. Here we see beautiful public buildings, churches, and fine stores. On some of the streets, we notice crowded sidewalk cafés and gay, open-air flower shops. Wherever we go, we hear people speaking Spanish.

**São Paulo.** From Buenos Aires, we fly northeastward to São Paulo, Brazil. Less than a hundred years ago this city was only a small community. Today, São Paulo is the leading industrial center and the largest city in South America. Nearly six million people live in São Paulo.

An abundant supply of hydroelectric power has helped São Paulo become a great manufacturing city. Much of the cotton cloth made in Brazil comes from São Paulo's textile factories. Steel, machinery, cement, shoes, and chemicals are only a few of the many other products that are manufactured here.

When we visit São Paulo, we learn that coffee is also important here. This city is located near the great coffee-growing region of southeastern Brazil. Roads and railroads connect São Paulo with rich farmlands farther inland and with the famous "coffee port" of Santos on the coast. Packing, hauling, and shipping the millions of tons of coffee grown in this region provide jobs for many people in São Paulo.

**Rio de Janeiro.** When it is time to leave São Paulo, we board an airliner and fly eastward to Rio de Janeiro.

Soon we see a tall, cone-shaped rock called Sugarloaf Mountain. This rock stands at the entrance to one of the most beautiful bays in the world. The Portuguese explorer who first saw this great bay on January 1, 1502, thought that it was a river. He named it Rio de Janeiro, or "River of January." Later, the small Portuguese settlement that grew up on the western shore of this bay also took this name. Today, nearly four and one-half million people

**Rio de Janeiro** is South America's second largest city. Its harbor is one of the best in the world.

live in Rio de Janeiro. It is the second largest city in South America.

As we near Rio de Janeiro, we see green, wooded hills and mountains. On one of these mountaintops, we notice the huge statue of *Christ the Redeemer* standing with arms outstretched above the city. After our plane lands, we decide to visit this mountain, which is called Corcovado. From its peak we look down on the city's parks and modern buildings. In the harbor below us are ships from many parts of the world.

Rio de Janeiro is one of Brazil's main ports. Here, products from the interior of Brazil and from other ports along the coast are loaded onto oceangoing ships and sent to other countries. We see men loading cargoes such as coffee, iron ore, cotton, and lumber. Ships carrying products which Brazil imports from other countries, such as wheat, machinery, chemicals, and petroleum, also come to this busy port.

**Brasília.** A six-hundred-mile plane ride from Rio de Janeiro brings us to Brasília, the capital of Brazil. (See map on page 61.) Below us, we see wide boulevards and modern buildings gleaming in the sunlight. More than half a million people live in this city.

Since colonial days, Brazilians had talked about moving their capital to the interior of the country. They thought a new capital city in the sparsely populated interior would help their country develop more quickly. In 1822, José Bonifácio, a Brazilian statesman, suggested the new capital be called Brasília. Years passed but little work was done. Then in 1956, Juscelino Kubitschek became president of Brazil. He promised the people that his government would build Brasília.

The site for Brasília was chosen, and a company was formed by the government to build the city. Then a contest was held to determine the best plan for the new capital. Many thousands of workers helped to build the new city. Although construction continues in the city even today, Brasília officially became the capital of Brazil in 1960.

After our plane lands at Brasília's airport, we ask a taxi driver to show us the city. Driving along a wide boulevard of a residential section, our taxi passes some modern apartment buildings. These are built in groups called superblocks. We leave the boulevard and drive closer to one of them. In this superblock, there are about a dozen apartment buildings, a school, and some stores. When Brasília is completed, there will be more than one hundred superblocks like this one.

Nearby, we see the Chapel of Our Lady of Fatima with its graceful, curving roof. We stop outside for a moment to listen to the music that is being broadcast from a tower close to this church.

Next, our taxi driver takes us to the Plaza of the Three Powers. Here we see Brazil's modern government buildings. Rising high above the plaza are the twin skyscrapers in which Brazil's lawmakers have their offices. Finally, we drive a short distance to the shore of a manmade lake to see the Palace of the Dawn, the home of Brazil's president.

**Lima.** Now we leave Brasília and fly westward across the continent to one of South America's oldest and most historic cities. This is Lima, the capital of Peru. Lima is a busy commercial and industrial city of about two and one-half million people. It is located in the desert, near the Pacific Ocean. A river flowing down from the Andes supplies

**Brazil's modern government buildings** are located in the capital city of Brasília. Why did the Brazilian people want to build this all-new city in the interior of their vast country?

water for Lima and for irrigated farmlands nearby. Cotton grown on these farmlands is woven into cloth in Lima's textile factories. Other factories make glassware, soap, and a variety of food products. Lima also has tanneries and oil refineries.

In Lima we see many reminders of the city's historic past. Founded in 1535 by Francisco Pizarro, Lima was an important trading city of the Spanish colonies in South America for many years. During our visit, we see several churches and other buildings that were built by the Spaniards. We also see the University of San Marcos, one of the oldest universities in all of North and South America.

# 8 Arts

**A Problem To Solve**
Many different groups of people make their homes in South America. Like people in other parts of the world, they enjoy music, painting, and other forms of art. How do the arts of South America reflect the varied backgrounds of the people who live on this continent? To solve this problem, you will need to find information about the backgrounds of the people who live in South America. Then you will need to make hypotheses about how their backgrounds are reflected in South American architecture, painting, literature, and music.

**See Skills Manual, pages 2-5**

**Architecture.** The oldest buildings in South America were built by the Indians. Let's travel to the land of the Incas to see some of these buildings. Northwest of Cuzco, Peru, lie the ruins of an old stone city called Machu Picchu. After lying hidden under dense undergrowth for about four hundred years, Machu Picchu was discovered in 1911 by a North American explorer, Hiram Bingham.

To reach Machu Picchu, we travel by train to the foot of the mountain on which the city was built. Then we ride up the mountain in a car to reach the ruins. Stone stairways connect the terraces on which the Incas built their houses, temples, storerooms, and fountains. From the lowest level to the highest, there are more than three thousand steps. Some of the stairs are in the open. Others lead through dark passageways.

One stairway brings us to a sundial carved out of a huge rock.

The Incas were remarkable engineers and builders. Some of the stone blocks they used in the buildings weigh fifty tons. We do not know exactly how they were able to move these great boulders and fit them together so perfectly.

Now let's travel northwestward to the city of Quito, Ecuador, to see some beautiful old churches. Many of the churches

The ruins of Machu Picchu, near Cuzco, Peru, are a fine example of the style of architecture developed by the Inca Indians hundreds of years ago. What are some of the different styles of architecture that have been used in South America during more recent years?

here and in other South American cities were built in the days when the countries of South America were colonies of Spain and Portugal. Most of these early churches were built in Spanish and Portuguese styles of architecture. Indian and mestizo* craftsmen carved and painted many of the decorations for the church facades and interiors. Much of this artwork was done in European style, but we also see Indian figures and designs.

The largest church in Quito is the Church of San Francisco. This famous church was built where an Inca palace stood long ago. The inside of this church is decorated with paintings, statues, and carved paneling. Wooden statues of the twelve apostles were carved and painted by a famous Indian wood-carver. Shining gold and silver decorate the high altar and columns at the front of the church.

*See Glossary

Many of the new buildings in South America's large cities are designed in modern styles. Brazil is one of South America's leaders in modern architecture. The Culture Palace in Rio de Janeiro has been called one of the most beautiful buildings in the world.

**Painting.** For a long time after the Spanish and Portuguese came to South America, the artists of South America painted delicate, pretty pictures in the styles of European painters. It was only recently that South American artists began to paint in a style of their own, using rich colors to paint bold pictures of people in their own countries. In Peru, Ecuador, and Bolivia, artists have cre-ated colorful, vigorous paintings of the Indians. Brazilian artists have painted pictures of Negro people. The west wall of the Culture Palace in Rio de Janeiro is decorated with a mural* by the famous Brazilian artist Cândido Portinari. This mural shows workers in some of Brazil's leading industries. In one panel, we see workers carrying large trays of coffee beans. Another panel shows stooped figures picking cotton. In paintings such as these, Portinari and other South American artists show the joys, the sorrows, and the problems of the people on the continent.

**Literature.** Ever since the days of the conquerors, South America has had many

*Coffee Carriers* is one panel of a mural painted by Brazilian artist Cândido Portinari. What are some of the things Portinari and other South American artists have tried to show in their works?

writers. The early explorers wrote about their adventures in this exciting new world. They also described the land and its people. One of South America's early writers was Garcilaso de la Vega. He was the son of an Inca princess and a Spanish soldier. We can read interesting stories and legends of the Incas in his *Royal Commentaries.* From these books, we learn about early Inca festivals and ceremonies, and about the suffering of the Incas under the Spanish conquerors.

Many authors have written exciting stories and poems about the life of the gauchos* who lived on the plains of Argentina and Uruguay. The most popular of these poems were written by José Hernández, who grew up among the gauchos. People in Argentina still enjoy Hernández's poems about Martín Fierro, the gaucho hero.

Today many South American authors write about the people of their countries who are poor or unhappy. Some of their novels and short stories are about people who live in crowded city slums. Others tell about people who struggle for their living in tiny villages high in the mountains, or in the forests of the lowlands. Through such stories, the writers try to point out some of the problems and needs of their people.

**Music.** It is evening high in the mountains of Peru. We are sitting on a hillside overlooking a broad valley. As we enjoy the beauty of the towering mountains and the quiet valley below, we hear a sad and lonely melody. Looking around us, we see an Indian boy walking down the hill with his llama. The boy is playing a *quena,* or reed flute. Perhaps this sad tune is one that was first played by his Inca ancestors long ago.

Now we go to a tiny village in central Chile. As we approach the village, we hear the gay, spirited music of the *cueca,* Chile's favorite dance. We hear people shouting and clapping their hands in time with the music. As we come closer, we see a young man dressed in Chilean cowboy clothes dancing with a beautiful girl in the center of the group.

Next we travel to a village on the northeastern coast of Brazil, where we hear a very different kind of music. The strange rhythms of this music came from the jungles of Africa. In colonial times, Portuguese settlers brought Negro slaves from Africa to work on their plantations. When these slaves came to South America, they brought the music and dances of Africa with them. Their rhythms and melodies gradually blended with the songs of their new homeland, and created a new kind of South American folk music.

Many modern South American composers have used the rhythms and melodies of folk songs in their music. At a concert in Rio de Janeiro, we listen to music by the famous Brazilian composer Heitor Villa-Lobos. In his composition *Amazonas,* we hear many of the folk tunes he had heard as a young man. During his lifetime, Villa-Lobos collected over five thousand Brazilian folk melodies and rhythms.

South Americans enjoy music and dancing. Throughout South America, people enjoy singing folk songs. They also play guitars and other instruments. In the concert halls of the larger cities, we may listen to South American symphonies and operas played by fine orchestras. Many of these musical works are well known and enjoyed in other parts of the world.

# 9 Crafts

For hundreds of years, the people in South America made by hand almost everything they used. They made their own clothing, furniture, rugs, dishes, and baskets. Today, in many villages, people still make almost everything they use. Some of these people even use the same kinds of tools their ancestors had long ago.

**Lacemaking.** In Paraguay, a short distance from Asunción, is the lacemaking town of Itauguá. Almost all the nanduti lace made in South America is made in this small town.

Nanduti is an Indian word for spider web. Legend says that delicate nanduti lace got its name from the work of an Indian woman long ago. Using her silver hair, she copied the delicate design of a spider's web. The result of her careful work was the first piece of spider-web lace.

In Itauguá we see many different patterns of this lace. Some pieces of lace are made in a star pattern and others are made in patterns of corn blossoms or other flowers. Sometimes it takes five years to finish one piece of lace. When it is finished, we may see this delicate lace on the high altar of a great cathedral. Sometimes the lace mantillas which women use to cover their heads when they go to church are made of nanduti lace. This lace is also made into collars, cuffs, and tablecloths.

**Weaving.** The Inca Indians were excellent weavers. Some of the fabrics made by the Incas were as finely woven as cloth made by modern methods. People living in the mountains today still make most of their clothing at home. Using wool from their own animals, they weave colorful ponchos, blankets, and other articles. Some of the most famous weavers are the Indians of Otavalo, Ecuador.

For a long time the Otavalo Indians used Inca designs in their weaving. Then the manager of a nearby plantation

Exchange

See pages 130-134

Pottery and other handmade articles are often sold in open markets in South America, as shown in the picture at left. Craftsmen who make these articles usually specialize in one craft, such as pottery or weaving. Why is it necessary for these craftsmen to sell or exchange the articles they make? Would they be able to meet the needs of their families if they did not carry on trade? Give reasons for your answers.

asked them to copy a piece of British tweed. The weavers did their work well, and soon they had more orders for this cloth. Today the entire valley around Otavalo has become a famous weaving center. Much of the cloth which the Indians make is woven in English and Scottish patterns to sell to tourists. Shawls, blankets, and fine Indian ponchos are sold in the market at Otavalo. Cotton cloth, pottery dishes, and many other Indian products are also for sale here.

**Straw hats.** Ecuador is famous as the center for weaving Panama hats. These straw hats are called Panama hats because many men going to California in the gold rush of 1849 bought these hats in Panama. In some towns in Ecuador, weaving these hats is the lifetime work of many people.

Panama hats are made from the fan-shaped leaves of the toquilla*plant. The leaves are cut while they are green, and soaked in boiling water to whiten them. After the leaves have been cut into narrow strips, the weavers begin their work. Through the open doorways, we may see people weaving the damp strips into hats. Sometimes they dip their fingers in water to keep the strips from breaking. Usually the people do the weaving in the early morning and in the evening, while the air is damp. It takes from one

*See Glossary

Weaving fabrics (left) and weaving straw hats (below) are two useful South American crafts. What kinds of articles are made by hand in the United States? How do you think the development of industry has affected crafts in the United States? Why are so many things still made by hand in South America?

week to three months to complete one hat.

**Handmade articles are sold in many shops.** Many other articles which are made by craftsmen throughout South America are sold in the cities. We can buy brightly colored pottery horses, small guitars, or tiny boxes lined with rabbit fur. Some shops sell fine leather handbags, wallets, and gloves. Others sell different kinds of trays, plates, and ornaments decorated with bright-colored butterfly wings. Many shops also sell special cups and straws made of silver, which are used for drinking maté. Maté is a popular tea drink in the southern part of South America.

**The Need
for Faith**

See pages 135-136

**During a religious festival in Cuzco, Peru,** a man in the costume of an Inca is carried in a procession. Many of South America's festivals are religious celebrations. Through the parades, plays, and music of these festivals, South Americans have an opportunity to express their faith in God. Do you think it is important for people to have opportunities to express their religious faith? Give reasons for your answer.

# 10 Festivals

**The Day of the Kings.** It is January sixth, the Day of the Kings, and you and I are in the city of Cuzco, Peru. This is a holiday in Cuzco and in many other parts of South America. On this day people celebrate the time long ago when the Three Kings, or Wise Men, brought their gifts to the Baby Jesus.

Outside our hotel, the streets of Cuzco are crowded with noisy throngs of people. Indian men and women are hurrying along the streets to the square in front of the Church of San Blas. We follow them to see the celebration.

When we reach the square, we join hundreds of excited people. Soon we see statues of the Virgin and the Baby Jesus swaying back and forth as they are carried through the crowds. People are beating drums, and banners are flying. Some of the Indians drop to their knees as the procession goes by.

After the procession has reached the square, a play begins on a high platform in front of the church. Wicked King Herod sends three soldiers into the crowd to kill any baby boys they can find. In this way he hopes to kill the Baby Jesus. Some of the people are carrying dolls made of paper. The soldiers find these dolls and pretend to kill them. However, they cannot find the Baby Jesus.

After the soldiers have finished their part of the play, the Virgin and Child appear on the platform. Then the Three Kings and their pages arrive. One of the kings is dressed as a Spanish conqueror. Another wears the costume of an Inca.

The third king is dressed as a man from Ethiopia. All the kings and their pages make speeches in honor of the Child. One of the pages is so excited that he jumps up and down and leaps about.

When this part of the play is over, Indians dressed in Inca costumes appear. They dance as the Inca Indians did long ago.

In some villages high in the Andes Mountains, about a third of the days of each year are devoted to festivals, or fiestas. Fiestas are an important part of the life of the people. Usually one person from the village is chosen to lead each fiesta. He plans the fiesta with his committees, and pays for most of the fireworks, music, and food for the whole village. Sometimes these celebrations are very expensive.

**Village market days.** During the time when the Incas ruled the towns and villages in the Andes, three days were set aside every month as market days. Today many towns and villages in the mountains have a market day each week. Let's visit Pisac, Peru, on Sunday to see what one of these Indian markets is like.

On Sunday morning we drive from Cuzco to Pisac. (See map on page 61.) When we reach the marketplace, we

**Indian mayors in Pisac, Peru.** Mayors from surrounding villages attend church services in Pisac on Sunday morning. After the services, they all march to the priest's house to receive his blessing.

find many Indians already displaying the goods they have brought to trade or sell. There are handwoven blankets, Indian hats, and handmade pottery. We see baskets piled high with tomatoes, melons, and other fruits and vegetables. There is even ice cream for sale. We stop and buy some llama-skin slippers that were made by an old Indian.

Stopping in front of a potato dealer, we notice that the potatoes he has for sale are quite different from those sold in the United States. These potatoes are about as big as ping-pong balls. The dealer tells us how he prepared the potatoes. First he froze them, and then he rubbed the skins off with his feet. Finally, he dried the potatoes into these small, white lumps.

Sunday in the town of Pisac is also famous for its parade of Indian mayors. Mayors from the surrounding villages come into Pisac on Sunday morning for church services. They march into town followed by young men who serve as their helpers. Each mayor carries a silver-trimmed staff made of dark, polished wood. This is the symbol of his authority. After the mayors have attended church services, they march to the priest's house to receive his blessing.

**Carnival.** We are now in the city of Rio de Janeiro, Brazil, far away from the Andes Mountains. Each year this city has one of the gayest Carnival celebrations in all South America. For four nights and three days before Lent, the people of Rio, and thousands of others who join them from all over the world, become Carnival merrymakers.

On the Saturday before Ash Wednesday, shopkeepers and businessmen close their stores and offices at noon. People go home to change into Carnival costumes. By six o'clock, Rio's gaily decorated streets and squares are filled with people who are laughing and shouting. Almost everyone is wearing a costume. Some people are dressed as clowns. Others are dressed as Roman senators, or pirates. Almost anything will do for a Carnival costume.

As we go out into the streets to join the crowd, we feel a cold shower of perfume. When the liquid hits us, it feels like hundreds of tiny icicles. Part of Carnival fun is squirting people with perfume.

As we follow the crowds through the streets of Rio, we notice that some songs are played over and over again. A man in the crowd explains the custom to us. Shouting above the din, he tells us that composers write new songs for Carnival every year. A few of these songs become Carnival favorites, and radio stations, bands, and orchestras play them over and over again.

After a night of celebrating Carnival, we return to our hotel in the early hours of the morning. By the time we get up later in the day, street cleaners have already swept away the confetti left from the celebrations of the night before. By early evening the streets are crowded again with merrymakers.

On the second night of Carnival, we go to President Vargas Avenue to watch people from some of the samba schools parade. The samba schools are organizations of people who enjoy dancing and having a good time at Carnival. All year long these schools plan and rehearse for the big samba schools' parade. About half a million spectators gather along President Vargas Avenue on the second

night to watch them. About fifteen thousand people march in the samba schools' parade.

Each samba school has a band, several floats, and hundreds of dancers for its part of the parade. As each samba school finishes, people rush out into the street. They throw confetti and shower perfume on each other. They pound on drums, rattle tambourines, and clang bells. When the police have cleared the streets again, the next dance group begins.

Monday night, the third night of Carnival, we visit some of the costume balls and parties held throughout Rio de Janeiro. Everywhere we go, we see hotels and halls packed with excited people. At the ball at the Teatro Municipal there is a contest to choose the best Carnival costume.

On the last day of Carnival, we watch another big parade that takes place during the evening. Some of the colorful floats we see during the parade depict events in Brazil's history. Others illustrate songs or famous people.

After this parade, Carnival comes slowly to an end. Tomorrow is Ash Wednesday, the first day of Lent. It is a holiday, a day of rest for the people of Rio. On Thursday everyone will return to work.

**Holy Week.** The next stop on our journey of festivals is the city of Popayán, Colombia. It is Holy Week, the last week of Lent. People come to Popayán from all over Colombia to see the Holy Week processions.

The first procession that we see is on Tuesday of Holy Week. A little before seven o'clock in the evening, we arrive at the Church of San Agustín. There we see the candlelight procession forming in front of the church. One by one, thirteen heavy statues are carried out of the church into the street. Each of the statues is on a richly decorated platform. These platforms are carried by men dressed in dark-blue robes. Carrying a statue in the Holy Week processions is an honor which sometimes has passed from father to son for hundreds of years in Popayán families.

As the procession moves, street sweepers walk in front of the procession to clear the way. Then come four little boys dressed in purple robes. One of the

**Samba dancers** parade during Rio's Carnival celebration. Dancers practice all year long for their part in this parade.

boys rings a small bell. Two of the others swing incense burners. The fourth little boy carries a crucifix. Men and women carry huge candles, four or five feet tall, that light the way for the procession.

As we watch the procession pass by, one of the men in the crowd tells us to watch for the statue called *The Master*. This statue is a large image of Christ wearing a crown of thorns. As it passes by, we are told that the people of Popayán think of this statue as the guardian of their city. They feel that it will protect their city from earthquakes, lightning, and termites.

Soon we see the last statue in the procession approaching us. This is a beautiful statue called *Our Lady of Sorrows*.

**Dancing Devils** perform in a street parade during one of South America's colorful festivals.

This statue is almost always carried last in Popayán's Holy Week processions.

**Corpus Christi Day.** Now it is early June and we are in Venezuela visiting the town of San Francisco de Yare, south of Caracas. It is Corpus Christi Day, a holy day for Roman Catholics. We are eating our breakfast when suddenly we hear firecrackers exploding in the street outside. Rushing outdoors, we see many people standing in the street and on the plaza. The Dancing Devils are coming.

The Dancing Devils of San Francisco de Yare are members of a religious society. They dance in the Corpus Christi Day festival to honor their Lord. We see that they are dressed in red costumes. Huge masks cover their heads. They wear rosaries,* and on their chests are small crosses of palm leaves. Each devil is rattling a maraca* and waving handkerchiefs fastened to a stick.

As the Dancing Devils come down the street, they do all sorts of tricks. When they reach the church, they stop and kneel very quietly. While the service is going on inside, they remain kneeling at the doorway. When the service is over, the festival begins again. Someone rings the church bells, other people pound on drums, and the devils rattle their maracas and dance. When the dance has ended, the devils scatter and visit important people of the town.

In the afternoon the crowd gathers again as the Corpus Christi Day procession moves through the streets. The devils dance as the procession passes, but they never turn their backs on the procession. Soon after the procession returns to the church, the music stops and the dancers are still. They kneel and throw their masks on the ground.

*See Glossary

**A park in Santiago, Chile.** City families in South America often like to spend Sunday afternoon strolling along the city streets, visiting friends, or enjoying a beautiful park.

# 11   Sports and Recreation

We are sitting in a small sidewalk café in Buenos Aires. At tables nearby, people are drinking coffee or eating ice cream. It is a warm Sunday afternoon. Several families are strolling along the sidewalk in front of the café. Some are on their way to visit relatives or friends. Others are going to spend the afternoon at one of the city's beautiful parks.

The people at the table next to ours are talking about the soccer game they are going to see tonight. We decide to go to the game too. Soccer, or *fútbol* as South Americans call it, is the most popular sport in South America.

**A soccer game.** In the evening we join a crowd of happy people who are going into the soccer stadium. When we reach our seats, high in the grandstands, we have an excellent view of the brightly lighted playing field far below us. It looks much like a football field in the United States. Two teams come onto the field. There are eleven men on each team. Now the game begins. One of the players kicks the ball toward the goal at the opposite end of the field. Another hits the ball with his head. The goal-keepers are the only players who are allowed to use their hands and arms to stop the ball.

Soon after the second half begins, the Buenos Aires team makes a goal. The people around us jump to their feet, shouting and cheering. Before long we, too, are cheering with thousands of excited spectators. When the game ends, we are happy that the home team has won.

**A bullfight in Lima.** It is a week later, and we are watching a bullfight in Lima, Peru. We are sitting with a crowd of people in one of the oldest arenas in South America. The matador, in his gold-embroidered jacket and satin trousers, is alone in the ring with the bull.

At a bullfight in Colombia. Bullfighting is not allowed in some South American countries. Why?

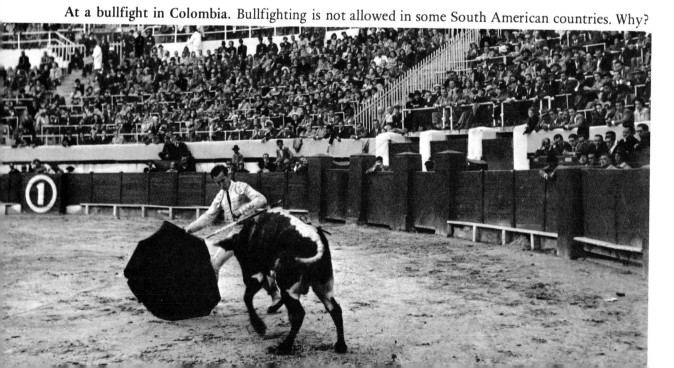

**A soccer game in Argentina.** More South Americans enjoy watching or playing soccer than any other sport. How does this sport help the people of South America meet their physical and social needs?

The matador skillfully and gracefully waves a short, red cape back and forth to attract the bull's attention. The bull charges at the red cape, first from one side, then from the other. The arena echoes with the cheers of the crowd. Finally, the matador raises his sword and with a skillful thrust kills the bull. Many people in the stands throw flowers and coins into the ring to honor the matador.

On Sundays during the bullfight season, crowds fill arenas in Colombia and Venezuela, as well as in Peru. In some South American countries, however, bullfights are not allowed, for many people feel that bullfighting is a cruel sport.

**Jai alai.** In the evening, we watch a game of jai alai. Seats are provided for spectators on one side of the large, paved court. The other three sides are enclosed by high walls. The game we are watching is a doubles match. Each of the four players has a narrow, curved wicker scoop, called a cesta, strapped to his wrist. The server bounces the ball,

Skiing in Chile. People in Chile and Argentina enjoy skiing and other winter sports during the month of July. Explain how this is possible.

which is about the size of a baseball, and hurls it with his cesta against one wall of the court. One of his opponents catches the ball in his cesta and sends it back. Each man tries to place the ball so that the players on the other team will not be able to return it. Sometimes the ball goes back and forth so fast we can hardly see it. A man sitting near us tells us that the ball, which is very hard, sometimes travels 150 miles an hour. Jai alai, which was invented in Spain long ago, is often called the fastest game in the world.

**Water sports.** On Wednesday afternoon we drive to a summer resort on a sheltered bay along the seacoast near Lima. Many people are sunbathing on the warm sand, or sitting in the shade of bright-colored umbrellas. Children paddle in the shallow water near the shore, while their older brothers and sisters swim in deeper water. Farther out, water skiers skim along, towed by fast boats. Across the bay, sailboats from the yacht club are taking part in a regatta, or race.

**Winter sports.** We are vacationing in Santiago, Chile. It is July, which is the middle of winter in the southern part of South America. We board a special ski train that takes us to Portillo, a resort village in the Andes. Snow covers the mountainsides. In many places, it is piled in deep drifts. A frozen pond is dotted with the figures of skaters. In the distance we see toboggans speeding down a mountain slope. Skiers are also gliding down the nearby slopes. Many people from Europe and the United States come to resorts like this in the mountains of Chile and Argentina to ski while it is summer at home.

## Use Your Creative Abilities

To discover more about the way of life of the South American people, you and your classmates may wish to complete one or both of the following projects.

1. Paint a mural. Choose a South American country or territory and do research about its people and their way of life. Then paint a mural to illustrate your discoveries. You may wish to show how different groups of people dress, how they earn their living, and what kinds of sports they enjoy.
2. Hold an arts and crafts fair. Do research about arts and crafts in South America. Then find examples of South American paintings and handmade articles and display them at an arts and crafts fair. You may be able to borrow these objects from a museum or from people in your community who have visited South America. If you cannot obtain the actual articles, you may use photographs or drawings of them. Or, you may wish to make articles similar to ones made by South American craftsmen. Photographs and drawings can also be used to show South American architecture, dancing, and other arts. Books containing literature written by South Americans might be put on display. You may be able to obtain records of South American folk songs and other musical compositions.

## Make Discoveries About Soccer

Soccer is becoming more and more popular in the United States today. Imagine that you are a soccer player from Argentina who has been asked to explain this sport to the students in your classroom. Prepare a talk in which you tell:

1. how the game of soccer began
2. how it got its name
3. how the game is played
4. what kind of clothes soccer players wear
5. ways in which soccer is similar to and different from American football

As you do research about soccer, you may find other things that you want to explain to your audience. To make your explanation of the game clearer, you may wish to draw a diagram of a soccer field, showing each player's position. As you carry out this project, follow the guidelines given on pages 13-19 of the Skills Manual for finding information and preparing an oral report.

## Use Your Imagination

About fourteen million Indians in South America are descendants of people who lived on this continent before the Spanish and Portuguese arrived. Imagine that you have visited a group of South American Indians, either in the mountains or the lowlands. Write a letter to a friend describing these people and their way of life. Do research in this book and other sources before you begin to write. Use the following questions as a guide.

1. How do most of these Indian people earn a living?
2. How do these people dress?
3. What types of homes and communities do these people have?

## Explore a South American City

The large cities of South America are colorful, exciting places to visit. Choose one of the following cities and do research about it in this book and other sources.

Buenos Aires    São Paulo    Montevideo
Lima            Bogotá       Rio de Janeiro

List the facts you find about the city you choose and then write an interesting report to share with your class. The following questions will help guide your research. You will probably think of other information that you would like to include.

1. Where is this city located?
2. How large is it and why is it important?
3. What are some of the points of interest in this city?
4. What are some of the ways in which people of this city earn a living?

The suggestions on pages 13-18 of the Skills Manual will help you to locate the information you need and to write a good report.

# Part 4
# Earning a Living

Many factors help determine how people in South America and other parts of the world earn their living. What do you think some of these factors are? As you do research in Part 4, you may wish to discover answers to the following questions.

- What factors help determine the kinds of crops and livestock that farmers raise in different parts of South America?
- In what ways does the abundance of natural resources in South America help provide jobs for the people there?
- Why do only a small part of South America's people earn their living in industry?

Meeting
Needs

See pages 135-136

The people of South America earn their living in many different ways. For example, the fishermen shown at left are unloading a catch of shrimp. Other South Americans have jobs in agriculture, mining, industry, or business. How does working at these various jobs help the people of South America meet their needs? Why do you suppose some South Americans are able to meet their needs more easily than others? Do research to discover more about the different ways of earning a living in South America. Choose the type of job you would like best and imagine that you are earning your living in South America. Write a story about your job, describing how it helps you meet your needs and the needs of your family.

# 12 Farming

**A Problem To Solve**

The picture at right shows a farmer in Peru. Farming is the most important way of earning a living in South America. However, only about one fourth of the land here is used for raising crops or grazing livestock. Why is such a small proportion of the land in South America used for agriculture? The following questions suggest hypotheses that will be helpful in solving this problem.

1. How do the land features of South America affect farming?
2. In what ways does climate affect farming in different parts of this continent?
3. What facts about vegetation help to solve this problem?
4. What facts about farming methods used in South America help to solve this problem?

Pages 12-24 also contain information that will be helpful in solving this problem.

See Skills Manual, pages 2-5

Only about a fourth of the land in South America is used for raising crops or grazing livestock. Mountains, deserts, and forests make much of the land unsuitable for farming. Nevertheless, agriculture is very important in South America. More than half the workers on this continent earn their living by farming. Farm products bring in much of the money that the South American countries earn from exports.

To learn more about farming in this vast continent, we will visit some of the farming areas in the mountains, the highlands, and the lowlands. We will notice that the land and the climate in each place largely determine the kinds of crops and livestock the farmers raise.

# Farming in the Mountains

**Farming in the Andes Mountains.** The Andes Mountains extend along the entire western coast of the continent of South America. Most of this vast mountain region cannot be used for farming. In the north, dense rainforest covers many mountain slopes. On the low ranges of the far southern Andes are

snow-covered peaks and a few glaciers. Here the climate is cold and stormy. The western slopes of the Andes in Peru are dry. In northern Chile, the mountains are part of a barren desert. Many peaks of the Andes are more than 20,000 feet above sea level. At this elevation, it is too cold for crops to grow or livestock to graze.

Scattered throughout the Andes, however, are many fertile valleys and plateaus where the climate is mild enough for farming. Centuries ago, people settled on some of these fertile lands.

They cultivated the land and raised livestock. Some of these early farmers learned how to irrigate their crops with water from mountain streams. In some places, they built terraces on the mountain slopes to provide more level land for growing crops. They also learned which crops would grow best at different heights in the mountains.

Today, many kinds of crops are grown in the Andes. Warm-weather crops such as sugarcane and coffee are raised on the lower mountain slopes of Colombia and Venezuela. Far to the south, the climate

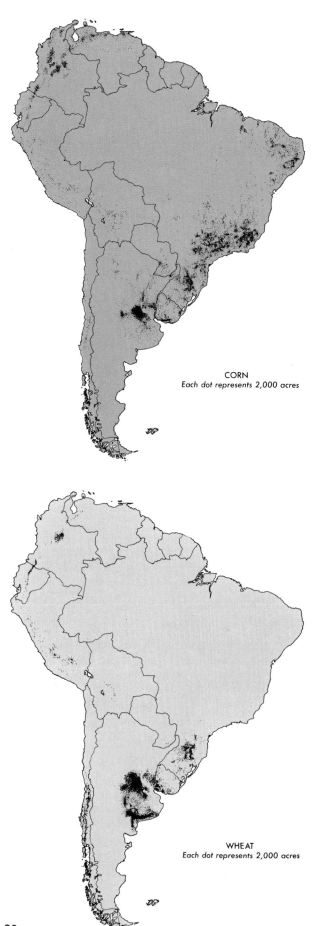

CORN
Each dot represents 2,000 acres

WHEAT
Each dot represents 2,000 acres

is not mild enough for these crops. In the valley of central Chile, farmers grow fruits, vegetables, and grain. High in the mountains of Peru, where it is too cold for crops to grow, cattle are grazed. Sheep, llamas,* and alpacas* graze on slopes that are too high for cattle.

**A train ride through southern Peru.** It is early in the morning, and our train has just left Arequipa, Peru. (See map on page 61.) We are traveling through a valley 7,500 feet above sea level. From the train windows we see fields of alfalfa, wheat, and corn. In this part of South America, these crops grow well at this elevation. We notice irrigation ditches in the fields. Because there is little rainfall the farmers must irrigate their land with water from mountain streams.

As our train travels higher, we notice that the air is much cooler. We are now more than 14,000 feet above sea level. The mountainsides are dotted with flocks of sheep, llamas, and alpacas. These animals graze on the coarse, wild grass and other plants that grow here.

We spend the night at the town of Juliaca, and continue our journey the next day. The train takes us northwestward through a range of snowcapped mountains. We notice that every available piece of land in the valleys and on the terraced mountainsides is being used for farming. Indians are working in fields of barley, potatoes, and wheat. Here in the mountains of Peru, the Indians work their farms much as their ancestors did many hundreds of years ago.

We descend from the high mountains to a broad, fertile valley about 11,000 feet above sea level. Here the irregular-shaped fields are bordered by gray stone walls. There are fields of corn, cabbages,

*See Glossary

and peppers, as well as fields of wheat and potatoes. From our train windows we catch glimpses of the ruins of Inca walls and buildings. As night falls, our train pulls into the city of Cuzco, once the capital of the Incas.

**Coffee in Colombia.** From Cuzco we fly northward to Colombia. (See map on page 9.) On some of the mountain slopes below us we can see row after row of trees that are growing on coffee plantations. The coffee trees, which are six or seven feet tall, are protected from the hot sun by tall shade trees. Colombia produces some of the world's best coffee. Most of this country's fine, mild coffee is grown on mountain slopes that are from 4,500 to 6,500 feet above sea level. Here the climate is ideal for growing coffee. The weather is warm, and plenty of rain falls at the right time of year.

COFFEE
Each dot represents 2,000 acres

# Farming in the Highlands

**Farming in the highland region.** The map on page 12 shows the three main highland areas of South America. In one of these, the Brazilian Highlands, farming is very important. Patagonia, in the far south, is a cool, windswept plateau which is used mainly for grazing sheep. There is almost no farming or grazing in the Guiana Highlands in the north.

SUGAR CANE
Each dot represents 2,000 acres

**Land rotation in Brazil.** Most of the farmers who live in the highlands north of the São Francisco River of Brazil are very poor. Some of them gather fibers and nuts from the wild plants and trees that grow there. They also collect the leaves of the carnauba* palm, which provide wax used in making floor polish, phonograph records, lipstick, and many other products.

Farming here is difficult and uncertain. This is partly because of the climate. During some years very little rain falls, and in other years there are floods. Also, poor farming methods have worn out the soil.

The farmer, who does not own the land, clears a few acres by cutting and then burning the trees and brush. For two or three years he farms for himself. The soil, which was fertilized by ashes from the burned trees, will grow corn, beans, cotton, and a few other crops. When crops no longer grow well, the farmer plants grass in the fields and moves on. The landowner then uses the cleared fields as pasture for cattle and goats, until brush and scrub trees once again cover the land. In the meantime, the farmer has begun to clear new land in the same way. In South America, this alternate clearing and abandoning of the land is called land rotation. Some of the land in the Brazilian Highlands has been cleared and abandoned so many times that the soil has become worn out and crops cannot grow on it.

One of Brazil's greatest resources is her land. The people are beginning to conserve and reclaim the worn-out soils by modern methods of flood control, terracing, and fertilizing.

**Picking coffee berries.** In which South American countries is coffee an important farm crop?

**Growing coffee in the Brazilian Highlands.** Although some of the soil in the southeastern part of the Brazilian Highlands has been worn out by land rotation, there are many fertile farming areas. Near the city of São Paulo is a coffee-growing region. Let us visit a coffee plantation, or *fazenda,* to see how coffee is grown in Brazil.

In São Paulo we board a train which takes us northwestward. Along the way we pass fields of cotton, corn, beans, and rice. Occasionally we see groves of orange trees, and cattle grazing in green pastures.

Finally, we reach the *fazenda.* The owner takes us on a tour of his plantation. As we walk through the groves of coffee trees, we notice that the soil is a

**Drying coffee berries in Brazil.** This country produces more coffee than any other nation in the world. What facts about the land and climate help to explain why coffee grows so well in Brazil?

reddish color. This is *terra roxa,* the fertile soil of much of Brazil's coffee country. This part of the Brazilian Highlands has an excellent climate for growing coffee. Ample rain falls during the long, warm summers, and the winters are short and usually frost free.

It is harvest season at the *fazenda.* Ahead of us we see women and children picking coffee berries from the lower branches of the trees. Some of the men have climbed ladders to reach the higher berries. Other workers are separating leaves and twigs from the berries by tossing them high into the air with wire trays.

At the *fazenda* headquarters other workers are busy spreading the coffee berries out in the sun to dry. For days,

and sometimes weeks, they rake the berries back and forth on drying floors. Each evening the workers rake the berries into piles and cover them with canvas so that dampness will not spoil them. When the berries are dry, they are put into machines that remove the outer husks that cover the coffee beans. About one third of the world's coffee is grown in Brazil.

**Sheep in Patagonia.** Patagonia is a bleak and barren plateau in southern Argentina and part of Chile. (See map on page 12.) The climate in most of Patagonia is too cool and too dry for raising crops. However, thousands of sheep graze on the wild grasses and scrubby bushes that grow in this area. During the mild summers and cooler winters the sheep grow thick fleece.

A cattle ranch in the Argentine Pampa. This vast, lowland plain is one of the best farming areas in the world. What kinds of crops and livestock do farmers and ranchers raise in the Pampa? What kinds of crops and livestock do farmers raise in other lowland areas on the South American continent?

## Farming in the Lowlands

**Farming in the lowland region.** Farming is important in three lowland areas of South America. One of these is a vast stretch of fertile land which includes the Pampa of Argentina and the plains of Uruguay. The others are the coastal lowlands of northeastern Brazil and the irrigated lands in the coastal desert of Chile and Peru.

There are also several lowland areas in South America where only a few people earn their living by farming. In vast stretches of the Amazon Lowland the soil is not good for growing crops. Also, it is difficult to clear the tropical trees

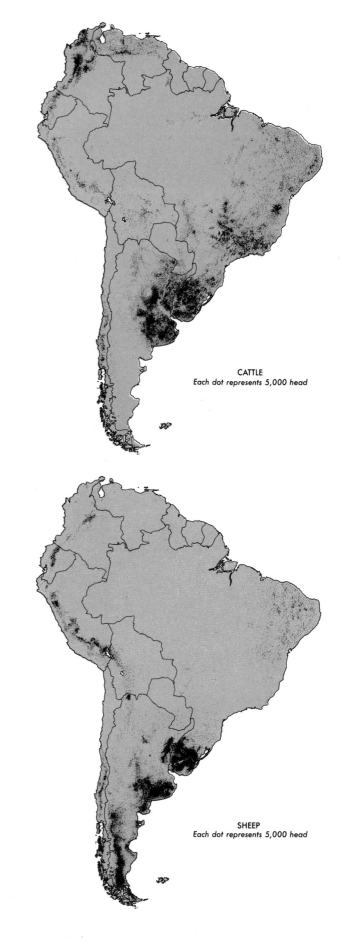

CATTLE
*Each dot represents 5,000 head*

SHEEP
*Each dot represents 5,000 head*

from the land. In the Gran Chaco and the Orinoco Llanos, some cattle are raised. However, only very hardy breeds of cattle can live here. Most of these cattle are sold for their hides.

**Farming in Argentina and Uruguay.** Let's visit a ranch on the Pampa of Argentina. At Buenos Aires we board a train for a trip westward. After our train leaves the city, we ride past fruit orchards and fields of vegetables. The produce of these small farms is grown to feed the people of Buenos Aires. Finally, we reach Argentina's cattle country. All around us we see cattle grazing on rich, green grass.

At the next station we leave the train. The manager of the ranch, or *estancia,* which we visit, provides us with horses. Soon we are riding through a huge pasture. Nearby, a windmill is pumping water for the cattle into long, metal troughs. Beyond the windmill, cattle are grazing as far as we can see.

Our host tells us that there are many pastures like this on the Pampa and on the plains of Uruguay. Some of them cover more than a thousand acres. In this part of the Pampa, most of the cattle are raised until they weigh about a thousand pounds. Then they are taken to railroad loading stations. From the loading stations, livestock trains take them to meat-packing plants on the coast. Meat is one of Argentina's chief exports.

The Pampa of Argentina is also one of the best wheat-growing areas of the world. At harvesttime, thousands of acres of golden grain stretch out across the land. The hot summers and rich soil of this area provide excellent conditions for growing grain. During the harvest season large combines* move through the wheat fields, cutting and threshing the grain as they go. Some of the farmers also grow other grains such as corn, oats, and barley.

**Warm-weather crops in Brazil.** Warm-weather crops such as sugarcane and cacao grow well in the tropical lowlands along the northeastern coast of Brazil. The days are hot throughout the year, and the rainfall is plentiful.

In the city of Salvador, we are met by a friend who owns a sugar plantation. Before long we are driving through fields of sugarcane on his plantation. The stalks of cane on either side of the road are so tall that we feel almost as if we are riding between high, green walls. Farther down the road, we see men cutting the tall stalks of cane and loading them onto wagons. These wagons take the cane to the sugar mill nearby.

At the sugar mill, we watch stalks of sugarcane being crushed between heavy rollers to press out the juice. In another part of the mill, this juice is heated and

passed through several different operations. This processing leaves brown crystals of sugar. The raw sugar is sent to a refinery, where it is made into fine, white sugar like we buy in stores. On some of the smaller plantations, the cane stalks are crushed between crude wooden rollers. The juice is boiled in pans over wood fires. The brown sugar formed by this process is called *rapadura*. It is sold in chunks to many people in Brazil, who use it just as it is.

Later, we visit a cacao plantation southwest of Salvador. Cacao beans, which are used to make cocoa and chocolate, grow only where the climate is hot and wet. They grow well in this part of South America, for it is hot and wet here throughout the year.

As we walk through the plantation, we notice that cacao trees have been planted in clearings in the forest. Some of the forest trees have been left standing to shade the young cacao trees and protect them from the wind. Sometimes we see banana plants growing among the cacao trees, for bananas also grow well in this hot, wet climate.

On the trunks and main branches of the cacao trees are bright-colored pods. Some of these are green, others are yellow, and still others are a purplish color,

Harvesting sugarcane. Warm-weather crops such as sugarcane and cacao grow best in a hot, wet climate. What parts of South America have a climate suitable for growing these crops?

for they do not all ripen at the same time. The workers ahead of us are picking only the ripe pods. Other workers cut these open with large knives and scoop out the cacao beans and the pulp which surrounds them. The beans and pulp are put into baskets and covered with banana leaves. They are allowed to stand for several days until the beans may be removed easily from the pulp. Then the beans are taken to large platforms and spread out in the sun to dry. Finally, the dried cacao beans are shipped to many parts of the world.

**Farming in the coastal desert of Peru and northern Chile.** Because it seldom rains on the desert that extends along the coasts of Peru and northern Chile, crops are grown only where the land can be irrigated. Farmers irrigate their fields with water from streams that flow down the Andes Mountains and cut across the desert to the sea. In the narrow river valleys, farmers raise sugarcane, cotton, and rice. Olives, grapes, and many other kinds of fruit are also grown here. Irrigation has turned these strips of barren desert into useful farmland.

**A grape harvest in Chile.** Many different kinds of fruit are grown in irrigated valleys along the coasts of Chile and Peru. Why is it necessary for farmers in these areas to irrigate their land?

## 13 Natural Resources

South America is rich in natural resources. Within this vast continent are rich mineral deposits, dense forests, and swiftly flowing streams. The forests and the mineral deposits provide raw materials for modern industries in many parts of the world. In some parts of the continent, waterpower from rivers is used to produce electricity for homes and factories.

**Petroleum.** The map on page 100 shows the main oil fields in South America. Although Venezuela has the richest oil fields on the continent, most of the other countries in South America also have important deposits of oil.

Venezuela is the fifth largest oil producer in the world. Nearly one tenth of the world's supply comes from this country. As we stand on the shore of Lake Maracaibo, we see row after row of tall oil derricks. Some of these derricks stand in shallow water. Others are

Oil drilling off the coast of Venezuela. This country is the fifth largest oil producer in the world. Do you think this natural resource has been a benefit to the people of Venezuela? Why do you think as you do?

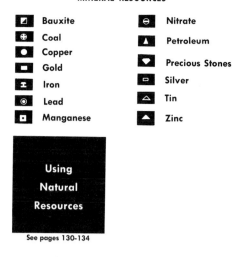

| | | | |
|---|---|---|---|
| ▨ Bauxite | | ⊖ Nitrate | |
| ⊕ Coal | | ▲ Petroleum | |
| ◖ Copper | | ▽ Precious Stones | |
| □ Gold | | ▭ Silver | |
| ⚎ Iron | | △ Tin | |
| ◉ Lead | | ◭ Zinc | |
| ▫ Manganese | | | |

**Using Natural Resources**

See pages 130-134

### A Problem To Solve

South America is rich in mineral resources, as shown on the map at left. However, large quantities of the ores mined in South America are not used on the continent. Why don't the people of South America make better use of their mineral resources? To solve this problem, you will need to consider the following:

1. ways in which minerals can be used to help people meet their needs
2. ways in which the ores mined in South America are used by the people who live there
3. development of industry in South America

See Skills Manual, pages 2-5

more than fifteen miles from shore in the deeper part of the lake. Altogether, there are more than four thousand wells in the oil fields of Lake Maracaibo. Some wells have been drilled down more than three miles under the lake.

Almost all the oil wells in Venezuela are operated by large foreign companies. These oil companies ship much of the oil to refineries in Venezuela or on the islands of Aruba and Curaçao off the coast. (See map on page 9.) Here it is made into fuel oil, gasoline, and other products.

Venezuela's vast deposits of oil have brought great wealth to the country. Although foreign companies operate most of the oil wells, they must pay the government of Venezuela more than three fourths of the profits they make from producing oil. With this money the government has built schools and hospitals, as well as roads and airports. Some of this money is also being used to help farmers learn new and better methods of farming.

Large deposits of natural gas have been found in the oil fields of Venezuela. Some of this gas is used in homes. Some provides fuel for factories.

**Iron ore.** In addition to oil, South America has large deposits of iron ore. (See map above.) About one third of the

**Mining iron ore** in the state of Minas Gerais, Brazil. This area of Brazil contains several billion tons of high-grade ore. What other South American countries have large deposits of iron ore?

world's iron ore reserves are in Brazil. The state of Minas Gerais, in the southeastern part of the country, has deposits containing several billion tons of high-grade iron ore.

Venezuela also has large deposits of iron ore. Most of this ore was discovered in the vast wilderness near the Orinoco River by men from steel companies in the United States. The largest deposit was found at Cerro Bolívar. This is a long, low mountain, with ore deposits four miles long and hundreds of feet deep.

Much work had to be done before any ore could be shipped from Cerro Bo-

lívar. Men and supplies were brought to this isolated region. A railroad was built from the mining area to the Orinoco River. Loading docks were built along the river. At first, the ore was loaded onto barges for shipment down the river to the coast. Finally, however, the river was dredged so that oceangoing freighters could reach the ore docks. Now millions of tons of iron ore are shipped each year to steel mills in the United States and Europe. Venezuela uses some of the iron ore in its own steel industry. An iron and steel plant located near the ore-loading area started production in 1962.

**Tin.** Bolivia is the world's second largest producer of tin. It is sometimes called the "land of tin." This country is the only large producer of this mineral in North or South America. Bolivia's tin mines are located high in the Andes Mountains. The highest of these mines is more than seventeen thousand feet above sea level.

It is difficult to transport Bolivia's tin ore from the mountain mines to the tin mills, which are in the valleys below. From some of the mines, the tin ore is carried by railroad to the mills. However, other mines are too far from railroads, so teams of mules or llamas carry the tin ore down the mountainsides. At the tin mills, some of the waste is removed from the ore. Much of Bolivia's tin ore is shipped to tin smelters* in the United Kingdom and the United States.

**Copper.** Chile is the world's largest producer of copper ore after the United States and the Soviet Union. Most of the copper ore which is mined in Chile comes from three major deposits, all located high in the Andes Mountains. (Compare map on page 100 with map on page 9.)

The largest copper deposit in the world is located at Chuquicamata, in northern Chile. Workers here mine the ore from an open pit on the rugged mountain slopes. Using explosives and huge power shovels, they cut back one level of the mountain after another in order to uncover the rich copper ore.

By comparing the map on page 100 with the map on page 9, we can see that there are also deposits of copper in Peru. The richest mining region is in the Andes east of Lima. The mines are from thirteen thousand to seventeen thousand feet above sea level. At this height, the air has much less oxygen than in the lowlands. People who are not used to the thin air find it very difficult to work at such heights. However, most of the miners are Indians who have always lived in the mountains and are able to live and work comfortably in the thin mountain air.

**Nitrate.** Nitrate is a mineral which is used as a fertilizer and as an important ingredient in making explosives. The largest deposits of nitrate in the world are located in the desert of northern Chile. For many years, Chile was the world's main source of nitrate. Then scientists discovered a way to make nitrate from the nitrogen* in air. Using this new process, factories in other countries began to manufacture nitrate. Hundreds of Chile's nitrate mines had to close. Today nitrate is still one of Chile's main exports, but less than one half of 1 percent of the world's nitrate comes from Chile.

South America has another resource which is valuable as a fertilizer. Millions of seabirds leave their droppings on the many small islands along the coasts of northern Chile and Peru. These droppings, called guano, contain nitrate, and are an excellent fertilizer for worn-out soil.

**Other minerals.** The map on page 100 shows us some of the other minerals that are found in South America. Large deposits of bauxite, the chief source of aluminum, have been found along the northern coast of South America in Guyana and Surinam. These are among the world's leading producers of bauxite. Brazil is a leading producer of manganese, an important mineral used in mak-

*See Glossary

**Nitrate mining in Chile.** The largest deposits of nitrate in the world are located in the desert of northern Chile. This mineral is one of Chile's main exports. In what ways is nitrate used?

ing steel. Large deposits of lead and zinc are mined in Peru.

There are small coalfields in almost all the countries of South America, but most of the coal is of poor quality. Much of the coal used in South America must be imported from other parts of the world.

Gold and silver have been mined in South America for hundreds of years. The map on page 100 shows us that there are still deposits of these minerals in some parts of South America. One of the world's deepest gold mines is the Morro Velho mine in the state of Minas Gerais, Brazil. This mine is more than one and one-half miles deep. Diamonds, emeralds, and other precious stones are also found in Minas Gerais. Most of the diamonds now mined in Brazil are black. These stones are used in factories for grinding, cutting, and polishing.

**Waterpower.** Waterpower is another important resource in South America.

Its many rivers could provide the waterpower for much of the electricity the continent needs. Until recently, however, very little of this waterpower has been used. It is very expensive to build the dams and power plants needed to produce hydroelectricity.* Also, many of the best locations for hydroelectric plants are far from the large cities where electricity is usually needed. Brazil is the leading producer of hydroelectric power, although Venezuela and other South American countries are using more and more of their waterpower to produce electricity for homes and factories.

**Fisheries.** Large numbers of fish live in the waters off South America's Atlantic and Pacific coasts. In recent years, important fishing industries have developed in South America. For example, Peru's yearly catch of fish is now the largest in the world. Most of the fish brought to Peruvian ports are anchovies. They are used mainly in the manufacture of fish meal and fish oil. Peru is the world's leading exporter of fish meal, which is used to make fertilizer and live-stock feed. Brazil, Chile, and Venezuela have also developed important fishing industries.

**Forests.** South America has many different kinds of raw materials in its vast forests. The largest rainforest in the world stretches across the Amazon Lowland from the Andes Mountains to the Atlantic Ocean. (See maps on pages 12 and 22.) Hundreds of different kinds of trees cover mile after mile of this vast lowland region. However, lumbering is not very important in the Amazon Lowland. Cutting and hauling trees in dense rainforest is usually very difficult and expensive.

The forests of the Amazon region do provide other valuable resources, however. Brazil nuts are an important export. They are good to eat, and they provide a fine oil as well. Other trees in the Amazon forest also yield oils for cooking or for making soaps and paints. Some plants have strong fibers that are used to make rope, cloth, and brushes. Medicines and waxes are made from other trees and plants that grow here.

Until about 1910, most of the world's rubber came from the Amazon Lowland. In some parts of the Amazon forest,

rubber trees are still tapped for their milky liquid, called latex. However, rubber plantations in other parts of the world can produce rubber much more cheaply than it can be produced in the Amazon forest. In addition, the use of synthetic rubber has increased throughout the world. As a result, little rubber is now collected in the Amazon Lowland.

In Argentina and Paraguay, there are forests of a strange kind of tree that grows nowhere else in the world. These trees are called quebracho, which means axbreaker. This wood is so hard that the axes used to cut down the trees must be made of special steel. Quebracho wood is a source of tannin, which is used in making leather.

Lumbering is also important in the southern Brazilian Highlands, where there are great forests of Paraná pine trees. Another product is maté, a kind of tea. Evergreen bushes, called yerba maté, grow in the shade of the pine trees. Maté, a popular drink in southern South America, is made from the dried leaves of these shrubs.

**Loggers in Brazil.** South America's forests provide many valuable raw materials. Name at least four of these raw materials and describe the kinds of products that are made from them.

# 14 Industry

South America's rich mines and forests provide many different kinds of raw materials for industries throughout the world. There are many factories in South America that also use these raw materials. However, only a small part of South America's people earn their living in factories or workshops. South America has not yet become a great industrial continent.

**South America's industrial cities.** If we travel to the city of São Paulo, Brazil, we can visit South America's leading industrial center. (See map on page 61.) São Paulo is a city of modern factories and skyscrapers. Office buildings, hotels, and department stores line the streets of the downtown area. Elsewhere in the city are large industrial districts where many modern factories are located. Many different kinds of products are manufactured here.

São Paulo became an important industrial center in South America for

FG-17

Division
of
Labor

See pages 130-134

**An assembly line** in an automobile plant in Brazil. Workers at each point along an assembly line perform different tasks that help complete the manufacture of a product, such as an automobile. Try to arrange for your class to visit a manufacturing plant in your area that has an assembly line. Before your visit, do research in other sources and prepare to discuss the following questions as a class.

1. Why do workers at different points along an assembly line perform different tasks?
2. Do you think manufacturers could have assembly lines without this division of labor? Give reasons for your answer.
3. What are some of the benefits of the assembly-line method of manufacturing?

The suggestions on pages 19 and 20 of the Skills Manual will help you to have a good discussion.

several reasons. Modern factories need power to run their machinery, and skilled workers to tend the machines. They also need efficient transportation to bring raw materials to the factories and to take manufactured goods to market. All of these are available in São Paulo. Power stations near the city supply inexpensive electric power to factories in São Paulo. Many skilled workers live in or near the city. A network of roads and highways connects the city with many of Brazil's rich mineral deposits and with inland coffee-growing plantations. A modern highway and a railroad also lead to the seaport of Santos. (See map on page 61.)

São Paulo is only one of several important industrial cities in South America. Rio de Janeiro, Buenos Aires, and Santiago are other leading industrial cities. These cities have modern industries which remind us of those in the United States and Europe.

**The textile industry.** The production of textiles and clothing is one of the oldest industries in South America. Hundreds of years ago, South American weavers made fine cotton and woolen cloth by hand. Today, South America has many textile factories. These factories use machinery to make cottons, woolens, and synthetic fabrics such as rayon and nylon. Some factories use jute* fiber to make burlap bags for coffee beans, grain, or other products.

High in the Andes Mountains, however, people still make almost all their textiles and clothing by hand. Indian women in the mountain villages spin the wool of llamas* into yarn just as the Inca women did long ago. These people buy very few things that have been made in factories.

**Food industries.** Industries which prepare food products provide work for many people throughout South America. Some of the people work in flour mills. Others work in canneries, sugar mills, or wineries. Many of the products made in these factories are consumed by South Americans.

In Argentina and Uruguay, meatpacking is one of the important food industries. Here American and British companies have built large meat-packing plants called *frigoríficos*. Cattle are brought to these *frigoríficos* to be butchered. Then the meat is canned, frozen, or chilled. Much of this meat is sold to countries outside of South America.

**The metal industry.** Another industry that is becoming more important in South America is the manufacture of iron and steel. Volta Redonda in Brazil is South America's largest iron and steel center. (See map on page 110.) Here are large, modern coke ovens and blast furnaces. Smoke pours out of tall chimneys. Freight cars shuttle back and forth bringing the raw materials needed to make iron and steel. The iron ore comes from mines only about 240 miles away. However, much of the coal used to make coke for the iron and steel industry at Volta Redonda is imported from the United States.

A large part of the steel made at Volta Redonda is shipped to factories in São Paulo and Rio de Janeiro to be made into metal goods. Skilled workers in these factories make products such

*See Glossary

**A textile mill in Lima, Peru.** What kinds of textiles are produced in South American factories?

**Using Tools**

See pages 130-134

Pouring molten iron at Volta Redonda, Brazil. Huge ladles, like the one shown in the top left of this picture, are used in iron and steel manufacturing plants. Such ladles, filled with molten iron or steel, are moved from one part of a plant to another by giant cranes. Do you think it would be possible to manufacture large quantities of iron and steel without the use of tools such as these? Why do you think this? Do research in other sources to discover information about some of the other tools that are used in manufacturing iron and steel.

South America has other steel mills. Venezuela has a mill on the Orinoco River near huge iron ore deposits. (Compare the map on this page with the maps on pages 9 and 100.) Peru and Colombia also have steel mills, and Argentina has several that use imported coal and iron. Uruguay, Paraguay, Bolivia, and Ecuador must import almost all of the iron and steel they use.

One of the important industries in South America that uses iron and steel is the automobile industry. Several European and North American automobile manufacturers have built factories in South America. In Brazil, for example, we can visit factories where cars are put together on modern assembly lines like those in the United States.

**The chemical industry.** The manufacture of chemicals is another important industry in South America. Factories in South America produce chemicals that are used in making products such as textiles, soaps, paints, and medicines.

**Industry is growing rapidly in South America.** Following the end of World War II, industry began to develop rapidly in South America. The governments of many South American countries helped businessmen establish factories. Large North American and European manufacturers also built many plants in South America.

Today, industry continues to grow rapidly in South America. However, many more mills and factories are needed to provide all the manufactured goods the people on the continent need. Industry is also needed to provide more jobs for the people of South America.

**South America's main industries.** What facts about natural resources, population, and transportation help to explain where industries in South America are located?

**INDUSTRIES**

- Chemical Products
- Food Products
- Forest Products
- Meat Industry
- Metal Industry
- Oil Refineries
- Textile Industry

as machinery, hardware, and kitchen utensils.

Another large iron and steel mill is located a few miles from Concepción, Chile. (See map on page 61.) This location was chosen because Chile's coalfields are nearby. The iron ore comes from mines about five hundred miles to the north.

**A chemical plant in Venezuela.** Factories in South America produce many different chemicals. Do research in other sources to discover what raw materials are used by the chemical industry.

Air transportation is very important in South America. What facts help explain why this is so?

# 15 Transportation and Communication

### A Problem To Solve

Why has it been difficult to develop good transportation and communication systems in South America? In forming hypotheses to solve this problem, you will need to consider the following:

1. land features and climates of South America
2. the size of railroad tracks in various South American countries
3. languages spoken in South America

See Skills Manual, pages 2-5

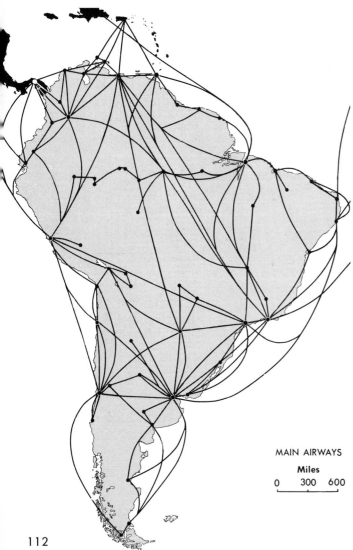

MAIN AIRWAYS

Miles

0    300    600

**An airplane trip across South America.** The sun is shining brightly at the airport near Lima, Peru. We board a large jet airplane for a flight across South America. Our trip from Lima to the city of São Paulo, Brazil, will take about four hours, for São Paulo is more than two thousand miles away.

Soon after we take our seats, our plane is flying over Lima. To our right, the blue waters of the Pacific Ocean extend to the horizon. The towering Andes Mountains rise on our left.

As we approach the Andes, we see the tracks of a mountain railroad. As we watch a train travel slowly up the

mountains, we can understand why air travel has become so important in South America. It is very costly and difficult to build roads and railroads through the mountains.

Now our stewardess announces that our plane is climbing higher to fly over the mountains. Some of the peaks we see from our plane window are more than twenty thousand feet above sea level. Even though it is summer, they are covered with snow.

After we have been flying for about an hour, we see a large lake below us. This is Lake Titicaca, one of the highest lakes in the world. It is on the border between Peru and Bolivia. At the southern end of the lake, we see a narrow pier extending out into the water. This is the southern terminal for the steamships that cross Lake Titicaca. These steamers were built in England and then were sailed to Peru. Here they were taken apart and carried up to the lake by mule and by railroad. Then they were put together again. Small reed boats are also used for transportation on Lake Titicaca. Indians living near the lake make these boats by tying reeds together with grass ropes.

As we continue our flight southeastward across Bolivia, we leave the high peaks of the Andes Mountains behind us. Near the border between Bolivia and Brazil we fly over the Paraguay River. This river is an important transportation route. São Paulo, our destination, is still more than 750 miles ahead.

Finally we approach the city of São Paulo, in the highlands of southeastern Brazil. This city is in a rich farming region. Networks of roads and railroads connect many towns with the city of São Paulo. When we land at the airport, we see planes from the United States, Europe, and many other lands. We also see planes of Brazilian airlines. These planes fly to many cities in South America. From the airport, we will travel by car to downtown São Paulo.

**Streets, roads, and highways.** São Paulo, like other modern South American cities, has wide streets that are busy with traffic. Broad avenues lead to the downtown section of the city. Some of these are bordered with tall trees, green grass, and flowers.

After we have lunch in São Paulo, we drive over a fine highway leading to the city of Santos on the coast. This modern concrete highway is called the Via Anchieta. It passes through tunnels and crosses deep valleys in the mountains as it winds down to the seacoast. The Via Anchieta is one of the best highways in South America.

Many of the roads in South America are narrow dirt trails. These dirt roads become very muddy when it rains. When it is dry, clouds of dust make traveling on these roads very unpleasant. Some roads have been covered with gravel or crushed rock to keep them from becoming muddy in wet weather.

A system of roads called the Pan American Highway connects the capital cities of all the South American republics. It also extends through Mexico and Central America. The only gap in the Pan American Highway is a 450-mile section in Panama and Colombia. When this is completed, it will be possible to drive from the United States all the way to Chile, Argentina, and Brazil.

**Railroads.** Only a small part of the continent of South America is served by railroads. The top map on the opposite page shows that most of the railroads have been built near the cities of Buenos Aires, São Paulo, and Rio de Janeiro. There is a large railway network branching out from each of these cities. Few railway lines extend east and west across South America. No railroad extends north and south through the whole continent.

Rio de Janeiro
São Paulo

Buenos Aires

MAIN ROADS
Miles
0    300    600

Pan American Highway

Railroads in South America differ so much from one another that it is very difficult to connect the various lines into a large system. One of the most serious problems is that the rails of some railroads are farther apart than those of others. In one country the railway tracks are spaced in five different widths. This makes it impossible for the trains of one railroad to use all the tracks in that country.

The railroads along the western coast of South America do not branch out in fan-shaped patterns from the main ports. Instead, most of them run north and south near the coast. A few railroad lines reach high up into the Andes Mountains. They are used mainly to bring minerals down from mines in the mountains to ports on the coast.

**Water travel in South America.** In some parts of South America, great rivers reach far into the interior of the continent. The lack of good roads and railroads in many places makes these rivers very important in the transportation system of South America. Riverboats and ocean steamers carry freight and passengers to many places.

The longest water highway in South America is the Amazon River, which flows from the Andes Mountains to the Atlantic Ocean. (See map on page 9.) In the harbor of Belém, near the Atlantic, we see ocean liners from many countries. Ocean vessels regularly sail from Belém to Manaus, about a thousand miles up the Amazon River. Some sail more than two thousand miles up the Amazon to Iquitos, Peru. (See map on page 61.) Smaller boats travel up the river for hundreds of miles beyond Iquitos.

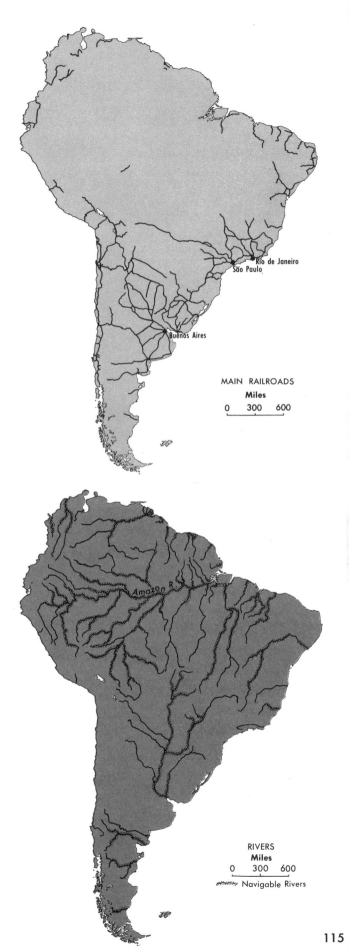

MAIN RAILROADS
**Miles**
0    300    600

Río de Janeiro
São Paulo
Buenos Aires

Amazon R.

RIVERS
**Miles**
0    300    600
Navigable Rivers

The Magdalena River in Colombia and the Orinoco River in Venezuela are two other important waterways in the northern part of South America. On the Magdalena, flat-bottomed riverboats carry freight and passengers from Barranquilla to La Dorada, a distance of about six hundred miles. Because the river is shallow and there are many shifting sandbars, boats are often delayed on this trip. Many of the boats on the Orinoco River are used to transport iron ore to the coast.

The most important rivers in the southeastern part of the continent are the Paraná, the Paraguay, and the Uruguay. The Paraguay flows into the Paraná River, which empties into the Río de la Plata,* near the city of Buenos Aires. Together, these rivers are about 3,500 miles long. The Uruguay, which also enters the Río de la Plata, is about one thousand miles long. Boats from Bolivia, Paraguay, Brazil, Argentina, and Uruguay travel up and down these rivers.

Coastal steamers are an important link in the transportation system of South America. Because overland travel in this continent is often slow and difficult, freight and passengers are transported by coastal steamers to many of the cities and towns along the coast.

**Communications.** It is often difficult for the people of South America to communicate with each other. Rugged mountains, dense forests, and great distances have made it difficult to string telephone and telegraph wires to all sections of the continent. Radiotelephone* and radiotelegraph* service to remote areas is helping to overcome these natural barriers.

The South American countries still need to improve their communication systems, however. Although South America has nearly as many people as the United States, it has only one twentieth the number of telephones. There are about two thousand radio stations and more than one hundred and fifty television stations on the South American continent. However, South Americans have far fewer radios and television sets than do people in countries such as the United States.

*See Glossary

**Filming a television program** in Venezuela. Most of the larger cities on the South American continent have at least one television station.

## Make a Farming Map

Many different kinds of crops are grown in South America. In some parts of the continent, large numbers of cattle and other livestock are raised. To discover more about farming in South America, make a map of the continent showing where different crops and livestock are raised. Draw in the three land regions of South America on your map and color them different shades. Then choose symbols for the crops and livestock you wish to show on your map. You will need to do research in this book and other sources to discover what South America's main crops and livestock are and where they are raised. After you have made a key and placed the symbols on your map, you may wish to share the map with your classmates.

## A Problem To Solve

South America has an abundance of raw materials for industry. However, only a small number of South America's people earn their living in manufacturing. Why has the development of industry been slow in South America? To solve this problem, you will need to make several hypotheses. (See pages 2-5 of the Skills Manual.) In forming your hypotheses, consider ways in which the following have affected the growth of industry here:

1. the availability of money to invest in industry
2. the availability of skilled workers
3. transportation facilities
4. the availability of power for factories

## Make a Minerals Chart

Do research about the mineral resources of South America and make a wall chart to hang in your classroom. As you do research, decide which of the minerals found in South America you want to include on your chart. Then discover the following information about each of the minerals you have chosen to investigate. List this information in appropriate columns on your chart:

1. countries in South America that have deposits of this mineral
2. the country that leads South America in the production of the mineral
3. how this country ranks among the other countries of the world in production of this mineral
4. uses of the mineral

## Plan an Imaginary Trip

If you compare the map on page 61 with the map on page 114, you can see that no main roads go directly from Quito, Ecuador, to Brasília, Brazil. If you were to journey between these two cities, you probably would not try to travel entirely by car. Imagine that you work for a travel agency and must plan a trip for a customer who wants to go from Quito to Brasília. Your customer would like to see some sights along the way. Use the maps and text in this book to plan an interesting trip. Then prepare a report for your customer, telling him about the route he will take, the sights he can see, and the forms of transportation he will use. In your report, explain to your customer why you have not planned a trip to be made entirely by car.

## Explore Relationships

Imagine that you are a businessman and are going to start a factory in South America. Select one of the following products to manufacture:

1. oil-drilling equipment
2. woolen cloth
3. copper wire

Decide where in South America you are going to build your factory. To make this decision, you will need to do research in this book and other sources to discover facts about the availability of the following:

| | |
|---|---|
| workers | transportation |
| power to run machines | raw materials |
| markets for your product | |

Summarize your reasons for your decision.

# Part 5

## Countries of
## South America

**São Paulo,** located on the eastern coast of Brazil, is South America's leading industrial center and the largest city on the continent. Nearly six million people make their homes in São Paulo.

# Argentina

**Land.** Lowlands make up about half of Argentina. In the east central part of the country is a vast plain called the Pampa. This region is one of the richest farming areas in the world. In the north are grassy, tree-dotted plains that are part of the Gran Chaco.

The rest of Argentina is made up of mountains and highlands. High ranges of the Andes extend along the western border. Mount Aconcagua, the highest peak in the Western Hemisphere,* is near the Chilean border. In southern

Argentina are the windswept plateaus of Patagonia.

**Climate.** Argentina's climate is more varied than that of any other South American country. On the snowcapped peaks of the Andes it is usually very cold. The climate of Patagonia is cool and dry. In the lowlands, winters are mild and summers are hot. The highest known temperatures in South America have been recorded in the Gran Chaco.

### Facts About Argentina

**Area:** 1,072,745 square miles.

**Population:** About 23,300,000.

**Density of Population:** 22 people per square mile; 301 people per square mile of arable* land.

**Capital and Largest City:** Buenos Aires (population about 3,447,000).

**Racial Composition:** More than three fourths of all Argentines are of European descent. Most of the rest are mestizo or Indian.

**Literacy:** About nine tenths of the people in Argentina can read and write.

**Main Language:** Spanish.

**Main Religion:** Roman Catholicism.

**Main Occupation:** About one third of the workers are employed in industry, mining, and construction. About one fifth earn their living in agriculture. Most of the rest have jobs in businesses that provide services to other people.

**Yearly Per Capita Income:** About $820.

**Important Farm Products:** Wheat, corn, linseed, alfalfa, rye, oats, barley, sunflower seeds, cotton, sugarcane, cattle, and sheep.

**Natural Resources:** Petroleum and salt are Argentina's main natural resources.

**Manufacturing:** Meat-packing, processing farm products, and textile manufacturing are the most important industries.

**Currency:** Argentina's unit of money is the *peso*, which is worth about 25 cents.

**Government:** A republic. In recent years the government has been under military control.

*See Glossary

Argentina, the second largest country in South America, has a great variety of land features.

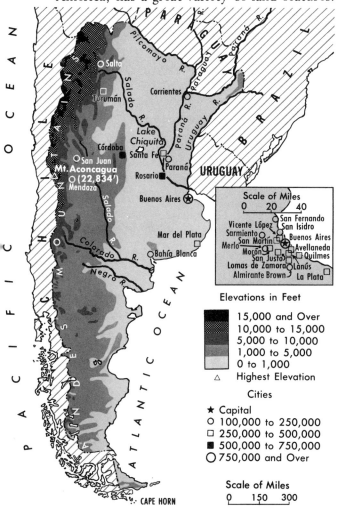

Elevations in Feet

- 15,000 and Over
- 10,000 to 15,000
- 5,000 to 10,000
- 1,000 to 5,000
- 0 to 1,000
- △ Highest Elevation

Cities
- ★ Capital
- ○ 100,000 to 250,000
- □ 250,000 to 500,000
- ■ 500,000 to 750,000
- ◯ 750,000 and Over

Scale of Miles
0    150    300

# Bolivia

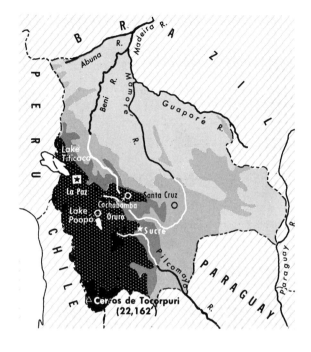

Elevations in Feet

| | |
|---|---|
| 15,000 and Over | |
| 10,000 to 15,000 | |
| 5,000 to 10,000 | |
| 1,000 to 5,000 | |
| 0 to 1,000 | |
| △ Highest Elevation | |

Cities

★ Capitals
○ 100,000 to 250,000
■ 500,000 to 750,000

Scale of Miles
0   100   200   300

Bolivia is made up mostly of rugged mountains and highlands. Lowlands lie in the northern and the eastern parts of the country.

**Land.** Bolivia is located in the west central part of South America. Unlike most countries of South America, Bolivia has no coastline. In the western part of Bolivia, the Andes are divided into two parallel ranges. Between them lies a bleak plateau called the Altiplano. The low plains in northern Bolivia are part of the Amazon Lowland. Lowlands in the east are part of the Gran Chaco.

**Climate.** In Bolivia the climate varies greatly from place to place. Days are warm in the lowlands the year around.

In the Altiplano, the climate is cold and windy. The average yearly temperature is only fifty degrees. High in the Andes, snow and ice cover the mountain peaks all year. Rainfall is light on the western mountain range and on the Altiplano. The northern part of the lowlands receives much more rain than the southern part.

## Facts About Bolivia

**Area:** 424,162 square miles.

**Population:** About 4,800,000.

**Density of Population:** 11 people per square mile; 301 people per square mile of arable* land.

**Capital and Largest City:** La Paz (population about 562,000) is Bolivia's administrative capital and largest city. Sucre (population about 58,500) is the judicial capital.

**Racial Composition:** More than half of the people of Bolivia are Indian. Others are descendants of Spanish conquerors who came to Bolivia long ago. About one third of the Bolivians are mestizo.

**Literacy:** About one third of the people of Bolivia can read and write.

**Main Language:** Spanish. Many Indians still speak their own languages.

**Main Religion:** Roman Catholicism.

**Main Occupation:** More than half of the workers earn their living by farming.

**Yearly Per Capita Income:** About $190.

**Important Farm Products:** Potatoes, corn, wheat, sugarcane, rice, and livestock.

**Natural Resources:** Bolivia is one of the world's largest producers of tin. Zinc, lead, copper, silver, petroleum, tungsten, antimony, and gold are other important resources.

**Manufacturing:** The leading manufactured products are textiles, foods, and beverages.

**Currency:** Bolivia's unit of money is the *peso*, which is worth about 8 cents.

**Government:** A republic. In recent years the government has been under military control.

*See Glossary

# Brazil

**Land.** More than one third of Brazil is made up of lowlands. The huge Amazon Lowland includes most of northern Brazil. The largest tropical rainforest in the world is in the Amazon Lowland. Narrow plains stretch along some parts of the Atlantic coast of Brazil.

Most of the southern half of Brazil is a vast region known as the Brazilian Highlands. This region consists of tablelands and rounded hills, with ranges of rugged mountains rising in several places. A small section of the Guiana Highlands extends along the northern border of Brazil.

**Climate.** The weather is never very cold in Brazil. Most of the country lies in the tropics.* At the equator, which passes through the Amazon Lowland, the temperature averages about eighty

Brazil is the largest country in South America and the fifth largest country in the world.

degrees all year round. In the highlands, it is generally cooler.

Rainfall is heavy in much of Brazil. Some parts of the Amazon Lowland and some areas along the Atlantic coast receive more than eighty inches of rain a year. Near the eastern tip of Brazil is an area where the average yearly rainfall is less than forty inches. Here, droughts sometimes destroy crops.

### Facts About Brazil

**Area:** 3,286,470 square miles.

**Population:** About 92,237,000.

**Density of Population:** 28 people per square mile; 992 people per square mile of arable* land.

**Capital and Largest City:** Brasília (population about 545,000) is the capital. Largest city is São Paulo (population about 5,901,000).

**Racial Composition:** More than seven out of every ten Brazilians are of European descent. About two out of ten are of mixed ancestry. Most of the rest are Negro or Indian.

**Literacy:** More than half of the people of Brazil can read and write.

**Main Language:** Portuguese.

**Main Religion:** Roman Catholicism.

**Main Occupation:** About half of the workers earn their living by farming.

**Yearly Per Capita Income:** About $440.

**Important Farm Products:** Coffee, cacao, cotton, rice, corn, sugarcane, jute, tobacco, beans, oranges, bananas, manioc, potatoes, wheat, hogs, and cattle.

**Natural Resources:** Iron ore, manganese, petroleum, gold, bauxite, salt, tin, coal, diamonds, other precious stones, forests, and fisheries.

**Manufacturing:** The leading products manufactured in Brazil are textiles, foods and beverages, cement, steel, chemicals, paper, and motor vehicles.

**Currency:** Brazil's unit of money is the *cruzeiro*, which is worth about 19 cents.

**Government:** A republic. In recent years the government has been under military control.

*See Glossary

121

# Chile

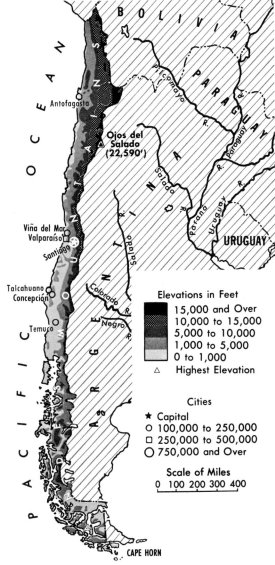

Chile is a narrow country that extends 2,650 miles along South America's Pacific coast.

**Elevations in Feet**
- 15,000 and Over
- 10,000 to 15,000
- 5,000 to 10,000
- 1,000 to 5,000
- 0 to 1,000
- △ Highest Elevation

**Cities**
- ★ Capital
- ○ 100,000 to 250,000
- ☐ 250,000 to 500,000
- ◯ 750,000 and Over

**Scale of Miles**
0 100 200 300 400

sands of rocky islands. Chile's main farming area is a fertile valley that lies between the low mountain ranges on the coast and the Andes on the east.

**Climate.** Chile has many different kinds of climate. In some parts of northern Chile, no rainfall has ever been recorded. Southern Chile is one of the wettest parts of South America. Much of this region receives more than 120 inches of rainfall each year. Central Chile has a pleasant climate with mild, wet winters and long, dry summers. In the high Andes, it is cold and snowy.

**Land.** Chile is a long, narrow country on the southwestern coast of South America. Along Chile's eastern border are high ranges of the Andes. Plateaus and low mountains lie along much of the Pacific coast. In southern Chile, the coastal plateau is broken up into thou-

### Facts About Chile

**Area:** 286,396 square miles.

**Population:** About 9,600,000.

**Density of Population:** 34 people per square mile; 386 people per square mile of arable* land.

**Capital and Largest City:** Santiago (population about 2,566,000).

**Racial Composition:** About two thirds of the people are mestizo. About two of every one hundred are Indian.

**Literacy:** About four fifths of the people in Chile can read and write.

**Main Language:** Spanish.

**Main Religion:** Roman Catholicism.

**Main Occupation:** About one third of the workers earn their living by farming.

**Yearly Per Capita Income:** About $761.

**Important Farm Products:** Wheat, oats, barley, rice, fruits, vegetables, cattle, sheep, and hogs.

**Natural Resources:** Copper, iron ore, nitrate, petroleum, coal, forests, and fisheries.

**Manufacturing:** The leading products manufactured in Chile are foods, beverages, textiles, clothing, chemicals, and steel.

**Currency:** Chile's unit of money is the *escudo*, which is worth about 8 cents.

**Government:** A republic.

*See Glossary

# Colombia

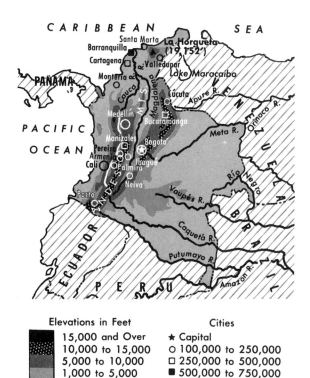

Colombia lies in the far northwestern part of South America. It is bordered by both the Pacific Ocean and the Caribbean Sea.

**Land.** About two thirds of Colombia is made up of lowlands. Swampy coastal plains extend along the Pacific Ocean and the Caribbean Sea. In eastern Colombia are grassy plains that are part of the Orinoco Llanos. (Compare map above with map on page 12.) Southeastern Colombia is part of the vast, forest-covered Amazon Lowland.

Three ranges of the Andes extend through the western part of Colombia. These high, rugged mountain ranges are separated by deep river valleys. Most of the people live in these valleys or in basins between the mountains.

**Climate.** In Colombia, temperatures vary mainly with elevation. The weather is usually cold on the high peaks of the Andes, but mild in the valleys. Most lowland areas are hot and humid. Rainfall is heavy in Colombia, especially along the Pacific coast. Some places here receive more than two hundred inches of rainfall every year. In the Orinoco Llanos, there is a dry season when little rain falls for several months.

## Facts About Colombia

**Area:** 440,505 square miles.

**Population:** About 21,100,000.

**Density of Population:** 48 people per square mile; 775 people per square mile of arable* land.

**Capital and Largest City:** Bogotá (population about 2,500,000).

**Racial Composition:** About seven out of every ten Colombians are mestizo. About two out of ten are white. The rest are Indian or Negro.

**Literacy:** About three fifths of the people of Colombia can read and write.

**Main Language:** Spanish.

**Main Religion:** Roman Catholicism.

**Main Occupation:** About half of the workers earn their living in agriculture.

**Yearly Per Capita Income:** About $303.

**Important Farm Products:** Coffee, bananas, sugarcane, cacao, corn, potatoes, rice, wheat, cotton, and cattle.

**Natural Resources:** Petroleum, gold, emeralds, iron ore, platinum, coal, salt, and forests.

**Manufacturing:** The leading products manufactured in Colombia are foods, beverages, textiles, clothing, chemicals, and steel.

**Currency:** Colombia's unit of money is the *peso*, which is worth about 5 cents.

**Government:** A republic.

*See Glossary

123

# Ecuador

**Land.** About three fifths of Ecuador is mountainous. Two high, parallel ranges of the Andes extend through the country. Between the mountains are fertile basins. East of the Andes are plains that are part of the Amazon Lowland. A low plain lies along the Pacific coast. Dense tropical forests cover most parts of Ecuador's lowlands.

**Climate.** In the lowlands of Ecuador, the climate is hot and humid. Rainfall is heavy in most areas. The basins of the Andes have a cool climate. Most of Ecuador's people live in these basins. On the high peaks of the Andes, it is cold and snowy.

### Facts About Ecuador

**Area:** 109,483 square miles.

**Population:** About 6,100,000.

**Density of Population:** 55 people per square mile; 719 people per square mile of arable* land.

**Capital and Largest City:** Quito (population about 530,000) is the capital. Largest city is Guayaquil (population about 790,000).

**Racial Composition:** Out of every ten people in Ecuador, about four are Indian, and about four are mestizo. Most of the rest are white or Negro.

**Literacy:** About seven tenths of the people of Ecuador can read and write.

**Main Language:** Spanish. Most Indians still speak their own languages.

**Main Religion:** Roman Catholicism.

**Main Occupation:** More than half of the workers in Ecuador earn their living by farming.

**Yearly Per Capita Income:** About $278.

**Important Farm Products:** Bananas, cacao, coffee, rice, sugarcane, barley, corn, potatoes, and livestock.

**Natural Resources:** Petroleum, gold, forests, and fisheries.

**Manufacturing:** The leading products manufactured in Ecuador are textiles, foods, drugs, chemicals, and petroleum products.

**Currency:** Ecuador's unit of money is the *sucre*, which is worth about 4 cents.

**Government:** A republic.

*See Glossary

Ecuador is one of the smallest countries in South America. It is in the northwestern part of the continent, on the Pacific coast.

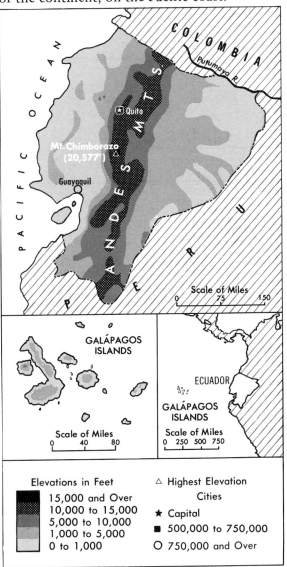

# French Guiana

**Facts About French Guiana**

**Area:** 35,135 square miles.

**Population:** About 45,000.

**Density of Population:** 1 person per square mile; 2,266 people per square mile of arable* land.

**Capital and Largest City:** Cayenne (population about 24,000).

**Racial Composition:** About 90 percent of the people of French Guiana are Negro or of mixed ancestry. Scattered groups of Indians live in the interior.

**Literacy:** About seven tenths of the people of French Guiana can read and write.

**Main Language:** French. A Guiana Creole dialect is also spoken.

**Main Religion:** Most of the people of French Guiana are Roman Catholic.

**Main Occupations:** Farming, fishing, mining, and lumbering are the main ways in which people in French Guiana earn their living.

**Yearly Per Capita Income:** About $840.

**Important Farm Products:** Bananas, rice, corn, manioc, sugarcane, and yams are the most important crops of French Guiana.

**Natural Resources:** Forests and gold are the most important natural resources. There are also valuable deposits of bauxite.

**Manufacturing:** Processing products from forests and farms is the leading industry in French Guiana.

**Currency:** French Guiana's unit of money is the *franc*, which is worth about 18 cents.

**Government:** An overseas department of France.

# Guyana

**Facts About Guyana**

**Area:** 83,000 square miles.

**Population:** About 740,000.

**Density of Population:** 8 people per square mile; 58 people per square mile of arable* land.

**Capital and Largest City:** Georgetown (population about 162,000).

**Racial Composition:** About half of the people of Guyana are of East Indian descent. About one third are Negro. Most of the rest are Indian or of mixed ancestry.

**Literacy:** About four fifths of the people of Guyana can read and write.

**Main Language:** English, Portuguese, East Indian, and local Indian dialects are spoken.

**Main Religions:** Christianity, Hinduism, and Islam.

**Main Occupation:** Many of the workers in Guyana are employed in raising and processing agricultural products. Some of the people work on large plantations and some on small farms. Other workers earn their living by mining, lumbering, or fishing.

**Yearly Per Capita Income:** About $430.

**Important Farm Products:** Sugarcane, rice, and coconuts are the leading agricultural products of Guyana.

**Natural Resources:** Bauxite, gold, diamonds, manganese, and forests are Guyana's most important natural resources. Guyana is one of the world's largest producers of bauxite, an ore from which aluminum is made.

**Manufacturing:** The leading products are processed foods and lumber.

**Currency:** Guyana's unit of money is the *Guyana dollar*, which is worth about 50 cents.

**Government:** A republic.

*See Glossary

125

# Paraguay

**Land.** Paraguay is located in the south central part of South America. Except for Bolivia, it is the only South American country without a coastline. The Paraguay River divides the country into an eastern region and a western region. East of the river are fertile lowlands and rolling hills. In the northeast is a plateau covered with dense, evergreen forest. West of the Paraguay River is a vast plain, which is part of the Gran Chaco. Most of this plain is covered with coarse grasses or tropical forest.

**Climate.** In Paraguay, the weather is warm most of the year. The average temperature is about eighty-five degrees during the summer months of December, January, and February. Temperatures sometimes reach 110 degrees in the Gran Chaco. During the winter, temperatures average about sixty degrees.

More rain falls in the eastern region of Paraguay than in the western region. The forested plateau in the northeast receives as much as eighty inches of rain a year. Rainfall is lighter in the Gran Chaco.

### Facts About Paraguay

**Area:** 157,047 square miles.

**Population:** About 2,395,000.

**Density of Population:** 15 people per square mile; 585 people per square mile of arable* land.

**Capital and Largest City:** Asunción (population about 437,000).

**Racial Composition:** Most of the people of Paraguay are mestizo.

**Literacy:** About seven tenths of the people in Paraguay can read and write.

**Main Language:** Spanish and Guaraní. Guaraní is an Indian language.

**Main Religion:** Roman Catholicism.

**Main Occupation:** More than half of the workers earn their living by farming.

**Yearly Per Capita Income:** About $231.

**Important Farm Products:** Manioc, rice, cotton, tobacco, sugarcane, corn, oil seeds, beef, and hides.

**Natural Resources:** Forests, which cover about half of the land, are Paraguay's main natural resource. Limestone is the only important mineral resource.

**Manufacturing:** The leading products manufactured in Paraguay are tannin, lumber, cement, beverages, meat products, and other food products.

**Currency:** Paraguay's unit of money is the *guarani,* which is worth less than one cent.

**Government:** A republic. Paraguay has been ruled by a dictator for many years.

*See Glossary

Paraguay is made up mostly of lowland areas. In the northeast is a forest-covered plateau.

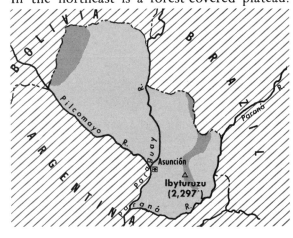

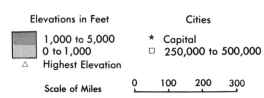

| Elevations in Feet | Cities |
|---|---|
| 1,000 to 5,000 | ★ Capital |
| 0 to 1,000 | □ 250,000 to 500,000 |
| △ Highest Elevation | |

Scale of Miles    0   100   200   300

# Peru

**Land.** Peru is located in the far western part of South America. It is bordered on the west by the Pacific Ocean. Three high ranges of the Andes extend through the western part of the country. Between the mountains are high plateaus and deep canyons. Along the Pacific coast is a narrow lowland. This part of Peru is a desert except where the land is irrigated with water from mountain streams. In the northeast are vast forested plains which are part of the Amazon Lowland.

**Climate.** The climate varies greatly from one part of Peru to another. In the coastal desert, it is generally warm and dry. Temperatures seldom go above eighty degrees. Although rain is rare here, days are often foggy or cloudy. In the mountains the climate is cooler, and the highest peaks are always covered with ice and snow. Rainfall on the low eastern mountain slopes sometimes exceeds 150 inches a year. In the northeastern lowlands, the weather is hot and rainfall is heavy all year long.

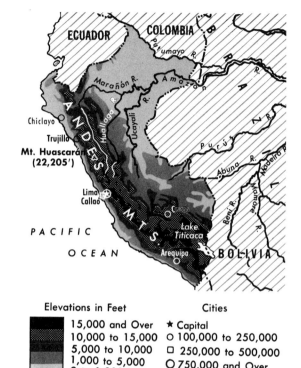

Elevations in Feet

15,000 and Over
10,000 to 15,000
5,000 to 10,000
1,000 to 5,000
0 to 1,000
△ Highest Elevation

Cities

★ Capital
○ 100,000 to 250,000
□ 250,000 to 500,000
○ 750,000 and Over

Scale of Miles
0  100 200 300 400

**Peru** is a land of towering mountains, deep canyons, high plateaus, and forested plains.

## Facts About Peru

**Area:** 496,222 square miles.

**Population:** About 13,586,000.

**Density of Population:** 27 people per square mile; 1,581 people per square mile of arable* land.

**Capital and Largest City:** Lima (population about 2,541,000).

**Racial Composition:** Almost half of the people of Peru are Indian. Most of the rest are mestizo.

**Literacy:** About three fifths of the people of Peru can read and write.

**Main Language:** Spanish. Indian languages are also spoken.

**Main Religion:** Roman Catholicism.

**Main Occupation:** About half of the workers earn their living by farming.

**Yearly Per Capita Income:** About $380.

**Important Farm Products:** Cotton, sugarcane, coffee, potatoes, rice, corn, barley, cattle, and wool.

**Natural Resources:** Fisheries, copper, lead, zinc, iron, gold, silver, tungsten, bismuth, antimony, guano, forests, and petroleum.

**Manufacturing:** The leading products manufactured in Peru are textiles, foods, beverages, chemicals, cement, fish meal, and leather and rubber goods.

**Currency:** Peru's unit of money is the *sol*, which is worth about 2 cents.

**Government:** A republic. In recent years the government has been under military control.

*See Glossary

# Surinam

## Facts About Surinam

**Area:** 55,144 square miles.

**Population:** About 400,000.

**Density of Population:** 7 people per square mile; 2,272 people per square mile of arable* land.

**Capital and Largest City:** Paramaribo (population about 135,000).

**Racial Composition:** More than one third of Surinam's people are Creole (mixed Spanish and Negro). More than one half are descended from settlers who came from India and Indonesia.

**Literacy:** About three fourths of the people of Surinam can read and write.

**Main Language:** Dutch. English is widely used in business in Surinam. Spanish and French are also spoken.

**Main Religions:** Christianity, Hinduism, and Islam.

**Main Occupations:** About one half of the workers in Surinam are employed either in agriculture or by the government.

**Yearly Per Capita Income:** About $380.

**Important Farm Products:** Rice is Surinam's leading export crop. Citrus fruits, sugar, and bananas are also exported.

**Natural Resources:** Bauxite and forests are the main natural resources.

**Manufacturing:** The leading manufactured products are foods and beverages, alumina, and wood products.

**Currency:** Surinam's unit of money is the *guilder*, which is worth about 50 cents.

**Government:** Partner in the Kingdom* of the Netherlands.

# Uruguay

## Facts About Uruguay

**Area:** 72,172 square miles.

**Population:** About 2,900,000.

**Density of Population:** 40 people per square mile; 305 people per square mile of arable* land.

**Capital and Largest City:** Montevideo (population about 1,400,000).

**Racial Composition:** Over four fifths of the people in Uruguay are of European descent. Most of the rest are mestizo or Negro.

**Literacy:** About nine out of every ten people in Uruguay can read and write.

**Main Language:** Spanish.

**Main Religion:** Roman Catholicism.

**Main Occupation:** About one half of the people in Uruguay earn their living in agriculture. About one tenth work in commerce, manufacturing, or government. Most of the rest are employed in construction or mining.

**Yearly Per Capita Income:** About $590.

**Important Farm Products:** Wool, meat, hides, wheat, corn, rice, citrus fruits, linseed, oats, and barley are Uruguay's leading farm products.

**Natural Resources:** Uruguay has few forests or other natural resources, except for marble and some small deposits of iron ore.

**Manufacturing:** The leading manufactured products in Uruguay are meat products, beverages, and textiles. The refining of imported petroleum is an important industry.

**Currency:** Uruguay's unit of money is the *peso*, which is worth less than one cent.

**Government:** A republic.

*See Glossary

# Venezuela

**Land.** Mountains and highlands cover much of Venezuela. In the northwestern part of the country are high ranges of the Andes. Low, parallel ranges extend eastward along the coast. South of Venezuela's largest river, the Orinoco, are the Guiana Highlands. Here are flat-topped tablelands and rounded hills, covered with forests.

Venezuela has two large lowland regions. One of these is in the northwest, around Lake Maracaibo. Between the Andes and the Guiana Highlands is the vast, grassy plain known as the Orinoco Llanos. (See map on page 12.)

**Climate.** The weather is usually hot in much of Venezuela. High in the Andes, however, it is cool all year round. During the dry season, vast areas of the Orinoco Llanos become brown and dry. Much of this great plain is flooded during the rainy season.

### Facts About Venezuela

**Area:** 352,143 square miles.

**Population:** About 10,400,000.

**Density of Population:** 30 people per square mile; 853 people per square mile of arable* land.

**Capital and Largest City:** Caracas (population about 2,000,000).

**Racial Composition:** About seven out of every ten Venezuelans are mestizo, and two out of ten are white. Most of the rest are Negro or Indian.

**Literacy:** About nine tenths of the people of Venezuela can read and write.

**Main Language:** Spanish.

**Main Religion:** Roman Catholicism.

**Main Occupation:** About one third of the workers in Venezuela earn their living by farming.

Other Venezuelans are employed in mining and industry.

**Yearly Per Capita Income:** About $940. This is the highest per capita income of any South American country.

**Important Farm Products:** Coffee, cacao, sugarcane, corn, rice, tobacco, sisal, bananas, and cattle.

**Natural Resources:** Petroleum, iron ore, diamonds, and gold.

**Manufacturing:** The leading products manufactured in Venezuela are textiles, clothing, foods, chemicals, drugs, and petroleum products.

**Currency:** Venezuela's unit of money is the *bolívar,* which is worth about 22 cents.

**Government:** A republic.

*See Glossary

Venezuela lies in the northern part of South America. It is bordered by the Caribbean Sea.

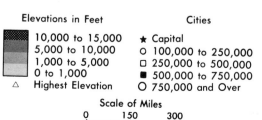

Elevations in Feet
- 10,000 to 15,000
- 5,000 to 10,000
- 1,000 to 5,000
- 0 to 1,000
- △ Highest Elevation

Cities
- ★ Capital
- ○ 100,000 to 250,000
- □ 250,000 to 500,000
- ■ 500,000 to 750,000
- ◎ 750,000 and Over

Scale of Miles
0    150    300

# Great Ideas of Man

Man has probably been living on the earth for more than two million years. During this time, man has met his needs in communities. No person can meet his needs by himself. Only by living and working with other people can he have a happy, satisfying life.

In order to make community life successful, man has developed certain ideas and ways of living. We call these the "great ideas of man." Let us examine nine of these great ideas and see how they have made it possible for man to live in communities.

**Cooperation.** In every community, people need to work together in order to accomplish their goals. Working together is called cooperation. Long ago, when most people were hunters, they had to cooperate closely to protect themselves from wild beasts and to get the food they needed. In what ways is cooperation important to communities today? What are some of the ways in which people cooperate with each other? What might happen to a community if people were not willing to work together?

**Rules and government.** Every community needs rules to guide the ways in which people act toward each other. Why is this true? What kinds of rules does your own community have? How do these rules make life safer and more pleasant for everyone? What would it be like to live in a community in which no one obeyed the rules?

In every community, there must be a person or a group of persons to make

the rules and see that they are carried out. In other words, all communities need some form of government. In what ways are all governments alike? How do governments differ from one another?

**Language.** In order to live and work together, people must be able to express their ideas and feelings to one another. The most important ways of communicating are by speaking and writing. Scientists believe that all human beings—even those who lived in earliest times—

**Schoolgirls in South America.** Children in South America obtain a large part of their education in school. In what other ways do you suppose young people make discoveries and learn new things?

have had some form of spoken language. Writing was not developed until about five thousand years ago.

How does language help you to meet your needs? What would you do if you could neither speak nor write? Would you be able to think and to solve problems without using language? Explain your answer.

**Education.** Another great idea of man is education. In every community, the older people pass on certain ideas and skills to the younger people. Would it be possible to have a successful community without education? Why? Why not?

In early times, parents taught their children most of the things they needed to know in order to live successfully. Today, children in most parts of the world obtain a large part of their education in school. Do you think education is important for every person? Why do you think as you do?

**Using natural resources.** In order to meet their needs, people in all communities make use of soil, water, air, sunshine, wild plants and animals, and minerals. These gifts of nature are called natural resources. Do you think a person would be able to meet his needs for food, clothing, and shelter without using natural resources? Give reasons for your answer.

In early times, people made little use of natural resources. Today, we use hundreds of them in many different ways. How have changes in the use of natural resources affected your life?

**Using tools.** A tool is anything that a person uses to help him do work. What kinds of tools do you use every day? In all communities, people use tools in meeting their physical needs. Would it be possible to have a successful community without tools? Why? Why not?

Tools that have a number of moving parts are called machines. Three hundred years ago, most machines were very simple. Then people began to develop more complicated machines. These could do many jobs that had formerly been done by hand. Today people use many different kinds of machines to produce goods. How do modern machines help people to meet their needs more successfully?

**Division of labor.** In every community, not all the people do exactly the same kind of work. Instead, they work at different jobs. For example, one man may earn his living by farming. Another man may be a baker and another may be a carpenter. Dividing up the work of a community among people who do different jobs is known as division of labor.

By using division of labor, people are able to obtain more goods than they could if each person tried to meet all of his needs by himself. What do you think are the reasons for this? Would it be possible to have a successful community without division of labor? Why? Why not?

A class at an agricultural school in Colombia. These students are learning how to use modern farm machinery. How might the use of machines, like the one shown in this picture, help them in farming? To answer this question, you may wish to do research in other sources about farm machinery.

133

**Exchange.** Whenever people divide up the work of a community, they need to exchange goods and services with each other. In this way, each person is able to obtain goods and services that he does not produce himself. What would it be like to live in a community where people did not use the great idea of exchange?

In early times, people did not carry on as much exchange, or trade, as people do today. We not only exchange goods and services within our own communities but we also carry on trade with people who live in communities far away. How does trade help people everywhere to have a better life?

**Loyalty.** In every truly successful community, most of the people are loyal to each other. They are loyal to the laws of their community and their country. They are also loyal to certain ideas and beliefs. In the United States, for example, most people are loyal to the principles of democracy. In addition, many people are loyal to their religious faith.

To what persons and ideas are you loyal? What are some of the ways in which you express your loyalty? How does loyalty help you meet your needs?

**Unloading cargo.** The people of South America exchange goods with people in many other parts of the world. Why do you think more trade is carried on today than was carried on in early times?

# The Needs of Man

The people of South America, like all other people on the earth, must meet certain basic needs in order to be healthy and happy. Scientists who study human behavior tell us that these basic needs are almost exactly the same for every person, whatever his skin color, his national origin, or his religion may be. Whether people are rich or poor, they have the same basic needs.

There are three kinds of basic needs. They are: physical needs, social needs, and the need for faith.

## Physical Needs

Some basic needs are so important that people will die or become seriously ill if they fail to meet them. These are called physical needs. They include the need for:

1. air
2. water
3. food
4. protection from heat and cold
5. sleep and rest
6. exercise

Although all people share these needs, they do not all meet them in the same way. How do you meet your physical needs? How do you think people in South America meet their physical needs?

## Social Needs

Each person also has social needs. He must meet these needs in order to have a happy and useful life. Man's social needs include the following:

**1. Belonging to a group.** Every person needs to feel he belongs to a group of people who respect him and whom he respects. Belonging to a family is one of the main ways people meet this need. What can the members of a family do to show that they love and respect each other? How do the members of your family help one another? Do you think family life is important to the people of South America? Why do you think this?

Having friends also helps people meet their need for belonging to a group. What groups of friends do you have? Why are these people your friends? Do you suppose young people in South America enjoy doing the same kinds of things with their friends as you enjoy doing with your friends? Why? Why not?

**2. Goals.** To be happy, every person needs goals to work for. What goals do you have? How can working toward these goals help you have a happy life? What kinds of goals do you think young people in South America have?

**3. A chance to think and learn.** Every person needs a chance to develop and use his abilities. He needs opportunities to find out about things that make him curious. What would you like to learn? How can you learn these things? How can developing your abilities help you have a happy life? Is it important for all people in South America to have a chance to think and learn? to make decisions for themselves? Why? Why not?

**4. A feeling of accomplishment.** You share with every other person the need for a feeling of accomplishment. Everyone needs to feel that his life is successful in some way. What gives you a feeling of accomplishment? Can you imagine what a person's life would be like if he never had this feeling?

## The Need for Faith

In addition to physical and social needs, every person also has a need for faith. He needs to believe that life is precious and that the future is something to look forward to. A person may have different kinds of faith, including the following:

**1. Faith in himself.** In order to feel secure, each person must have faith in his own abilities. He must feel that he will be able to do some useful work in the world and that he will be generally happy. He must believe that he can work toward solving whatever problems life brings to him. How do you think a person can build faith in himself?

**2. Faith in other people.** Every person needs to feel that he can count on other people to do their part and to help him when he needs help. What people do you have faith in? What do you

think life would be like without this kind of faith?

**3. Faith in nature's laws.** Another kind of faith that helps people face the future with confidence is faith in nature's laws. The more we learn about our universe, the more certain we feel that we can depend on nature. How would you feel if you couldn't have faith in nature's laws?

**4. Religious faith.** Throughout history, almost all human beings have had some kind of religious faith. Religion can help people understand themselves and the world they live in. It can bring them joy, and it can give them confidence in times of trouble. Religion can also help people live together happily. For example, most religions teach people to be honest and to love and help their neighbors. In what ways do people in South America express their religious faith?

## Many People in South America Are Unable To Meet Their Basic Needs

The 195 million people living in South America must meet the three kinds of basic needs we have explored here. They must meet these needs in order to have happy, useful lives. However, millions of South America's people do not have a chance to satisfy some of their important needs. For example, large numbers of them do not have enough food to eat or adequate shelter.

Why are so many people in South America unable to meet all of their needs? What is being done to help these people have a better life? Do research in this book to find information that will help you answer these questions.

# GLOSSARY

## Complete Pronunciation Key

The pronunciation of each word is shown just after the word, in this way: **alpaca** (al pak′ ə). The letters and signs used are pronounced as in the words below. The mark ′ is placed after a syllable with a primary or strong accent, as in the example above. The mark ′ after a syllable shows a secondary or lighter accent, as in **antimony** (an′ tə mō′ nē).

Some words, taken from foreign languages, are spoken with sounds that otherwise do not occur in English. Symbols for these sounds are given at the end of the table as "foreign sounds."

| | | | | | | | |
|---|---|---|---|---|---|---|---|
| a | hat, cap | j | jam, enjoy | u | cup, butter |
| ā | age, face | k | kind, seek | u̇ | full, put |
| ã | care, air | l | land, coal | ü | rule, move |
| ä | father, far | m | me, am | ū | use, music |
| b | bad, rob | n | no, in | | |
| ch | child, much | ng | long, bring | v | very, save |
| d | did, red | o | hot, rock | w | will, woman |
| | | ō | open, go | y | young, yet |
| e | let, best | ô | order, all | z | zero, breeze |
| ē | equal, see | oi | oil, voice | zh | measure, seizure |
| ėr | term, learn | ou | house, out | | |
| | | p | paper, cup | ə | represents: |
| f | fat, if | r | run, try | a | in about |
| g | go, bag | s | say, yes | e | in taken |
| h | he, how | sh | she, rush | i | in pencil |
| | | t | tell, it | o | in lemon |
| i | it, pin | th | thin, both | u | in circus |
| ī | ice, five | ŦH | then, smooth | | |

| foreign sounds | Y as in French *du*. Pronounce ē with the lips rounded as for English ü in rule. | N as in French *bon*. The N is not pronounced, but shows that the vowel before it is nasal. |
|---|---|---|
| | œ as in French *peu*. Pronounce ā with the lips rounded as for ō. | H as in German *ach*. Pronounce k without closing the breath passage. |

**Aconcagua** (ä′kôn kä′gwə), **Mount.** A mountain in the Andes of Argentina, 22,834 feet high. (See map, page 9.) It is the highest peak in the Western Hemisphere.

**alpaca** (al pak′ə). A domestic animal of the camel family, usually raised for its wool. It is smaller than a llama and larger than a vicuña. (See **llama** and **vicuña**.) Its fine, long, woolly hair is used to make lightweight cloth.

**Amazon.** See **Amazon River.**

**Amazon Lowland.** Lowland in northern South America. (See map, page 12.) Drained by the Amazon River and its tributaries.

**Amazon River.** The longest river in South America, about 3,900 miles long. Begins in the Andes Mountains and flows eastward into the Atlantic Ocean. (See map, page 9.)

**Andes Mountains.** Rugged mountain chain that extends along the entire western coast of South America. (See map, page 12.)

**Angel Falls.** The highest waterfall in the world. Located in southeastern Venezuela.

antimony (an'tə mō'nē). A hard, brittle, silvery-white metal. Often mixed with other metals to harden them.

appreciation. The understanding or awareness of the worth of something. For example, you may develop an appreciation for art or music. You may also develop an appreciation for the accomplishments of people of other cultures.

arable (ar'ə bl). Refers to land that is suitable for cultivating crops.

Araucanian (ar'ô kän'ē ən) Indians. Warlike Indians who lived in Chile hundreds of years ago. Also, their descendants who now live in the forests of southern Chile.

Arequipa (ä'rä kē'pä). A city in southern Peru. (See map, page 61.)

Argentina (är'jən tē'nə). The second largest country in South America. Located in the southeastern part of the continent. (See map, page 9.)

Aruba (ä rü'bä). A small island in the Caribbean Sea near the coast of Venezuela. Part of the Netherlands Antilles. (See map, page 9.) One of the world's largest oil refineries is located here.

Ash Wednesday. The first day of Lent. See Lent.

Asunción (ä sün syôn'). Capital city of Paraguay. (See map, page 61.)

axis. An imaginary line that passes through the earth, joining the North and South poles. It takes the earth about twenty-four hours to rotate once upon its axis.

Bahia (bə ē'ə). The name of a state in Brazil. Also, another name for the city of Salvador.

Barranquilla (bär'räng kē'yä). A port city on the Magdalena River in northern Colombia. (See map, page 61.)

bauxite (bôk'sīt). The ore that is the chief source of aluminum.

Belém (bə lem'). A port city on the Pará River, in northern Brazil. (See map, page 61.)

Bingham, Hiram, 1875-1956. North American senator, teacher, and explorer. Discovered the Inca city of Machu Picchu in 1911. See Machu Picchu.

bismuth (biz'məth). A grayish white metal. Often mixed with other metals so that they will melt easily.

Bogotá (bō'gō tä'). Capital of Colombia, located in the Andes Mountains. (See map, page 9.)

Bolívar (bō lē'vär), Simón, 1783-1830. South American soldier and statesman, known as the Liberator. Helped lead Spanish colonies in South America to independence.

Bolivia (bə liv'ē ə). Fifth largest country in South America. Located in the west central part of the continent. (See map, page 9.)

Bonifácio (bō nē fä'sē ō), José, 1763?-1838. Full name, José Bonifácio de Andrada e Silva. A leader in the Brazilian government in the early 1820's, both before and after Brazil gained its independence.

Brasília (brə zēl'yə). Capital city of Brazil. Located in the interior, about 600 miles from the coast. (See map, page 61.)

Brazil (brə zil'). Largest country in South America and fifth largest in the world. (See map, page 9.)

Brazilian Highlands. A large highland area located mainly in Brazil. (See map, page 12.)

Buenos Aires (bwā'nōs ī'rās). Capital and largest city of Argentina. (See map, page 61.)

Cabral (kə bräl'), Pedro Álvares, 1460?-?1526. A Portuguese navigator who claimed Brazil for Portugal on April 22, 1500.

cacao (kə kā'ō). Seeds from which chocolate and cocoa are made. Also refers to the tree on which these seeds grow.

Cajamarca (kä'hä mär'kä). A town located in the Andes Mountains of northern Peru. (See map, page 61.) Here Pizarro captured and killed the ruler of the Inca Indians.

Callao (kä yä'ō). Second largest city in Peru and seaport for the city of Lima. (See map, page 61.)

Cape Horn. A rocky point of land on Horn Island at the southernmost tip of South America. Often called the Horn. (See map, page 9.)

**Caracas** (kə rak′əs). Capital and largest city of Venezuela. Located in the northern part of the country. (See map, page 61.)

**Caribbean** (kar′ə bē′ən) **Sea**. An arm of the Atlantic Ocean that borders the western part of South America's northern coast. (See map, page 9.)

**carnauba** (kär nou′bə) **palm**. A Brazilian palm tree whose leaves are coated with wax. This wax is used to make floor polish, candles, and other products.

**centimeter** (sen′tə mē′tər). A unit for measuring length. It is equal to slightly less than one-half inch. The centimeter is a unit in the metric system of measurement. The metric system is used in most countries and by scientists throughout the world. In this system, 100 centimeters equal one meter, and 1000 meters equal one kilometer. A meter is about 39 inches in length, and a kilometer is equal to about two thirds of a mile.

**Chile** (chil′ē). A long, narrow country on the southwestern coast of South America. (See map, page 9.)

**Chuquicamata** (chü′kē kä mä′tä). A mining town in northern Chile. (See map, page 61.) The largest copper deposit in the world is located here.

**circumference** (sər kum′fər əns). The distance around an object or a geometric figure, especially a circle or a sphere.

**coca** (kō′kə). A shrub that grows in South America. The drug cocaine is obtained from its leaves.

**Colombia** (kə lum′bē ə). The fourth largest country in South America. Located in the northwestern part of the continent. (See map, page 9.)

**combine** (kom′bīn). A machine that cuts, threshes, and cleans grain while moving across a field.

**common market**. An association of countries formed to promote greater freedom of trade between the member nations and to help their industries grow. Member nations of a common market usually eliminate tariffs, or taxes, on most products shipped between them. Manufacturers are better able to sell their goods to customers in other common-market countries because the prices of these goods are lower. These manufacturers now have more money to use for expanding their industries. They are able to buy more machinery and provide more jobs for more workers. It is hoped that the Latin-American common market, by encouraging the growth of industry, will help to raise the standard of living in the member nations.

**compass rose**. A small drawing included on a map to show directions. A compass rose is often used as a decoration. Here are three examples of compass roses:

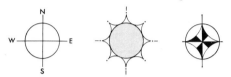

**Concepción** (kôn′sep syôn′). The third largest city in Chile. Located in central Chile. (See map, page 61.)

**crucifix**. A cross to which a figure representing the body of Christ is attached. Used as a Christian symbol.

**Curaçao** (kyùr′ə sō′). An island in the Caribbean Sea near the coast of Venezuela. Part of the Netherlands Antilles. (See map, page 9.) One of the world's largest oil refineries is located here.

**Cuzco** (küs′kō). A city located in a valley in the Andes Mountains of southern Peru. (See map, page 61.) Former capital of the Inca Empire. See **Inca Empire.**

**diameter** (dī am′ə tər). A straight line that goes through the center of a geometric figure, especially a circle or sphere. The line joins two opposite points on the figure.

**Ecuador** (ek′wə dôr). A country in northwestern South America. Named for the equator, which passes through the northern part of the country. (See map, page 9.)

**equator** (i kwā′tər). An imaginary line around the earth, dividing it into a northern half and a southern half.

**equinox** (ē′kwə noks). Either of two times of the year when the sun shines directly on the equator. These occur about March 21 and September 22. On these dates, day and night are of equal length everywhere on earth.

**estancia** (es tän′syä). Spanish name given to cattle ranches in parts of South America.

**fazenda** (fə zen′də). Portuguese name given to plantations in Brazil. Usually refers to coffee plantations.

**fiord** (fyôrd). A narrow arm of the sea that reaches far inland. Usually fiords are very deep and have steep sides.

**French Guiana** (gē an′ə). An overseas department, or political division, of France. It has two representatives in the French parliament. French Guiana is located on the northeastern coast of South America. (See map, page 9.)

**Galápagos** (gə lä′pə gəs) **Islands.** Group of islands belonging to Ecuador. Located in the Pacific Ocean, 600 miles west of Ecuador's coast. (See map, page 124.)

**Garcilaso de la Vega** (gär′sē lä′sō ᴛʜä lä vā′-gä), 1539?-1616. A Peruvian writer and historian.

**gauchos** (gou′chōz). South American cowboys famous for their horsemanship. Usually descendants of both Spanish and Indian peoples.

**Gran Chaco** (grän′ chä′kō). A lowland area in the central part of South America. (See map, page 12.) Includes parts of Argentina, Paraguay, and Bolivia.

**great circle.** Any imaginary circle around the earth that divides its surface exactly in half. The equator, for example, is a great circle. The shortest route between any two points on the earth always lies on a great circle.

**guano** (gwä′nō). Bird droppings found on certain islands and coasts. Used as fertilizer.

**Guayaquil** (gwä′yä kēl′). Main seaport and largest city of Ecuador. Located on the Guayas River, near the Pacific coast. (See map, page 61.)

**Guiana** (gē an′ə) **Highlands.** An area of rounded hills and flat-topped tablelands in northern South America. (See map, page 12.)

**Guyana** (gī an′ə). An independent nation, member of the British Commonwealth.

Located on the northeastern coast of South America. (See map, page 9.) Formerly the colony of British Guiana.

**Hernández** (er nän′dāth), José, 1834-1886. An Argentine poet, author, and newspaperman, famous for his poems about gauchos. See **gauchos.**

**hydroelectricity** (hī′drō i lek′tris′ə tē). Electricity produced by waterpower. The force of rushing water is used to run machines called generators, which produce electricity.

**Inca.** Title given to the ruler of the Inca Empire. See **Inca Empire.** Sometimes refers also to a person of the Inca Empire.

**Inca Empire.** An Indian empire which extended about 3,000 miles along the western coast of South America. Conquered by the Spaniards in the 1530's. (See map, page 33.)

**Inca Indians.** See **Incas.**

**Incas.** Indian people who lived in or near Cuzco and founded the Inca Empire. See **Cuzco** and **Inca Empire.** Also refers to other tribes conquered by these people and made a part of the Inca Empire.

**incense.** Fragrant substances burned to produce a pleasing smell, used especially in religious services.

**intermarried.** Intermarriage is marriage between people of different races or groups.

**Iquitos** (ē kē′tōs). A port city on the Amazon River in northeastern Peru, more than 2,000 miles from the Atlantic Ocean. (See map, page 61.)

**Itaugua** (ē′tou gwä′). A small town in southern Paraguay. (See map, page 61.) Center for making nanduti lace.

**jai alai** (hī′ ä lī′). A game played on a paved court with a hard rubber ball and narrow wicker baskets.

**João** (zhwouN), also **John VI,** 1769-1826. A Portuguese prince who fled to Brazil when Napoleon's army invaded Portugal. Became king of Portugal in 1816.

**Juliaca** (hü lyä′kä). A town in southern Peru. (See map, page 61.)

**jute.** A long, shiny plant fiber that is used to make burlap, twine, and other products.

**Kingdom of the Netherlands.** An association made up of the Netherlands and its two territories, the Netherlands Antilles in the Caribbean and Surinam in South America. See **Surinam.**

**Kubitschek** (kü′bə chek), **Juscelino** (zhü ′sə-lē′nü), 1901- . President of Brazil from 1956 to 1961. Under his leadership, the city of Brasília was built.

**La Dorada** (lä ŦHŌ rä′ŦHä). A river port and railroad town on the Magdalena River in western Colombia. (See map, page 61.)

**Latin America.** Includes Mexico and the parts of Central America, the West Indies, and South America where Spanish, French, or Portuguese is the main language.

**Lent.** A period of fasting observed by some churches before Easter.

**Lima** (lē′mə). The capital and largest city of Peru. (See map, page 61.)

**llama** (lä′mə). A domestic animal of the camel family. Used as a pack animal in the Andes Mountains. Its coarse wool is spun into yarn.

**Machu Picchu** (mä′chü pēk′chü). An ancient Inca city in the mountains of southern Peru. It was discovered in 1911 by Hiram Bingham. (See picture, pages 66 and 67.)

**Madeira** (mə dir′ə) **Islands.** A group of islands, located in the Atlantic Ocean off the northwestern coast of Africa. These islands belong to Portugal.

**Magdalena** (mäg′ŦHä lā′nä) **River.** A river in western Colombia. Begins in the Andes Mountains and flows northward into the Caribbean Sea. (See map, page 9.)

**Manaus** (mə nous′). A port city in western Brazil. Located on a tributary of the Amazon River, about 1,000 miles from the Atlantic Ocean. (See map, page 61.)

**manganese** (mang′gə nēs). A grayish white metal. Often used with other metals to make them harder and tougher.

**manioc** (man′ē ok). A tropical plant, which is also called cassava. Its roots look somewhat like sweet potatoes and are used for food.

**mantilla** (man til′ə). A covering for the head and shoulders worn by women in South America. Often made of black lace.

**maraca.** A rattle made of a dried gourd filled with pebbles or seeds. It is used as a musical instrument.

**Maracaibo** (mar′ə kī′bō), **Lake.** A large lake in northwestern Venezuela. It is connected by a narrow channel to an inlet of the Caribbean Sea. (See map, page 9.)

**Mendoza** (men dō′sə). A city in western Argentina in the foothills of the Andes Mountains. (See map, page 61.)

**Mendoza** (men dō′sə), **Pedro de,** 1487?-1537. A Spanish soldier and explorer. In 1536 he founded the first colony at Buenos Aires.

**Mercator** (mėr kā′tər) **projection.** One of many possible arrangements of meridians and parallels on which a map of the world may be drawn. Devised by Gerhardus Mercator, a Flemish geographer who lived from 1512 to 1594. On a Mercator map, all meridians are drawn straight up and down, with north at the top. The parallels are drawn straight across, but increasingly farther apart toward the poles.

**mestizos** (mes tē′zōz). People who have both Indian and European ancestors.

**Minas Gerais** (mē′nə zhā rīs′). A state in eastern Brazil.

**Morro Velho** (môr′ō vä′lyü). A gold mine in the state of Minas Gerais, Brazil. One of the deepest gold mines in the world. See **Minas Gerais.**

**mural** (myùr′əl). A decorative painting made directly on a wall.

**Napoleon** (nə pō′lē ən) **Bonaparte** (bō′nə-pärt), 1769-1821. A French general. Became emperor of France in 1804. Conquered most of Europe, but was defeated by combined European armies.

**nitrogen.** A colorless gas that forms about four fifths of the world's atmosphere. About one fifth of the atmosphere is oxygen.

**Northern Hemisphere.** The half of the earth's surface north of the equator.

---

PRONUNCIATION KEY: hat, āge, cãre, fär; let, ēqual, tėrm; it, īce; hot, ōpen, ôrder; oil, out; cup, pùt, rüle, ūse; child; long; thin; ŦHen; zh, measure; ə represents a in about, e in taken, i in pencil, o in lemon, u in circus. For the complete key, see page 137.

**O'Higgins, Bernardo,** 1778-1842. A Chilean soldier, called the Liberator of Chile. Ruled Chile from 1817 to 1823.

**orbit.** The path followed by the earth as it moves around the sun.

**Orellana** (ō'rä yä'nä), **Francisco de,** 1500?-1549. A Spanish soldier. Explored the Amazon River from the western part of South America to the Atlantic Ocean. (See map, page 33.)

**Orinoco** (ōr'ə nō'kō) **Llanos** (lä'nōz). Plains in northern South America between the Andes Mountains and the Guiana Highlands. (See map, page 12.)

**Orinoco** (ōr'ə nō'kō) **River.** A river in the northern part of South America. It begins in southern Venezuela and flows into the Atlantic Ocean. (See map, page 9.)

**Otavalo** (ō'tä vä'lō). A town in northern Ecuador. Center of an Indian weaving district. (See map, page 61.)

**Pampa** (pam'pə). Vast, grassy plain in Argentina. (See map, page 12.) One of the richest farming areas in the world.

**Panama hat.** A handwoven hat made from the leaves of the toquilla plant. See **toquilla.**

**Paraguay** (par'ə gwā). A small inland country in the south central part of South America. (See map, page 9.)

**Paraguay** (par'ə gwā) **River.** A river in the south central part of South America, about 1,500 miles long. Begins in southwestern Brazil and flows into the Paraná River. (See map, page 9.)

**Paraná** (pä'rä nä') **River.** A river in the southeastern part of South America. (See map, page 9.) Begins in Brazil and flows southward into the Río de la Plata. See **Río de la Plata.**

**Pará** (pə ra') **River.** Name of the eastern mouth of the Amazon River. (See map, page 9.) It is about 200 miles long.

**Patagonia** (pat'ə gōn'yə). A cool, dry plateau in the southern part of South America, between the Andes Mountains and the Atlantic Ocean. (See map, page 12.)

**Pedro, Dom,** 1798-1834, also **Pedro I.** A Portuguese prince who became the first emperor of Brazil. Ruled Brazil from 1822 until 1831.

**Pedro II, Dom,** 1825-1891. Emperor of Brazil. A wise and good ruler, his reign lasted until 1889, when Brazil became a republic.

**per capita income.** A country's per capita income is the total income of all the people divided by the number of people in the country. Per capita figures are often rough guesses, for it is difficult to obtain correct figures.

**Peru** (pə rü'). The third largest country in South America. Located on the western coast of the continent. (See map, page 9.)

**Pisac** (pē säk'). A small town in southern Peru, near Cuzco. (See map, page 61.)

**Pizarro** (pi zär'ō), **Francisco,** 1470?-1541. The Spanish explorer who conquered Peru.

**Pizarro** (pi zär'ō), **Gonzalo,** 1506?-1548. Spanish half brother of Francisco Pizarro. Traveled with Francisco to Peru, and later explored parts of Ecuador. See **Pizarro, Francisco.**

**plaza** (plä'zə). An open area, or square, in a town or city.

**poncho.** An outer garment made like a blanket with a narrow opening in the center for the head.

**Popayán** (pō'pä yän'). A city in southwestern Colombia. (See map, page 61.)

**Portillo** (pōr tē'yō). A village in the Andes of central Chile. (See map, page 61.) Famous as a center for skiing and other winter sports.

**Portinari** (pōr'tē nä'rē), **Cândido,** 1903-1962. A Brazilian artist whose paintings and murals often portray life in Brazil.

**quebracho** (kā brä'chō). A tropical tree with very hard wood that grows in Argentina and Paraguay. A source of tannin. See **tannin.**

**quinoa** (kē nō'ä). A plant that grows in the Andes Mountains. Seeds of this plant are ground and eaten as cereal.

**Quito** (kē'tō). Capital city of Ecuador. Located high in the Andes Mountains, about fifteen miles south of the equator. (See map, page 61.)

**radiotelegraph service.** A method of communication by which a series of radio relay towers transmits telegraphic signals without connecting wires.

**radiotelephone service.** A method of communication by which a series of radio relay towers transmits telephone calls without connecting wires.

**rainforest.** Commonly, a dense forest found in tropical areas that have no dry season and receive very heavy rainfall. A rainforest consists mostly of tall broad-leaved evergreen trees. See **tropical rainforest.**

**republic.** A country or state in which the people who may vote hold the power. They choose the men who will run their government.

**Rio de Janeiro** (rē′ō də jə nā′rō). Second largest city in Brazil, and an important seaport. Also the former capital of Brazil. (See map, page 61.)

**Río de la Plata** (rē′ō də lə plä′tə). An estuary, or arm, of the Atlantic Ocean between Argentina and Uruguay. The Paraná and Uruguay rivers empty into it. (See map, page 9.)

**Roman Catholic Church.** A branch of Christianity. The head of the Roman Catholic Church is called the pope.

**Roman Catholics.** Refers to members of the Roman Catholic Church.

**rosaries.** Strings of beads used by some Christians to count their prayers.

**Salvador.** An important seaport and trade center in Brazil. (See map, page 61.)

**samba.** A kind of Brazilian dance.

**San Francisco de Yare** (sän′ frän sēs′kō dā yä′rā). A small town in northern Venezuela. (See map, page 61.)

**San Martín** (sän′ mär tēn′), **José de,** 1778-1850. A South American statesman and soldier who helped Spanish colonies in South America win their independence.

**Santiago** (sän tyä′gō). The capital and largest city of Chile. (See map, page 61.)

**Santos** (san′təs). A port city built on an island near the southeastern coast of Brazil. (See map, page 61.) Exports more coffee than any other port in the world.

**São Francisco** (souɴ′ fraɴ sēsh′kü) **River.** A river in eastern Brazil, about 1,800 miles long. Flows into the Atlantic Ocean. (See map, page 9.)

**São Paulo** (souɴ′ pou′lü). The largest city in Brazil, and South America's leading industrial center. (See map, page 61.)

**São Vicente** (souɴ′ vē sänn′tə). A city in southeastern Brazil. (See map, page 61.)

**sisal** (sis′l). A plant from which a tough, white fiber is obtained. This fiber, which is also called sisal, is used to make twine and rope.

**smelt.** To melt ore in order to separate the metal from the waste material.

**smelters.** Places where metal ore is melted to separate the metal from the waste material.

**Solís** (sō lēs′), **Juan Díaz de,** 1470?-1516. A Spanish navigator. Was appointed pilot major of Spain in 1512. Discovered the Río de la Plata in 1516, where he was killed by Indians.

**solstice** (sol′stis). The time of the year when the sun is the farthest north or south of the equator. In the Northern Hemisphere, the summer solstice is about June 21 and the winter solstice is about December 22.

**Southern Hemisphere.** The half of the earth's surface south of the equator.

**square inch.** A unit for measuring area, equal to the area of a square that measures one inch on each side.

**standard of living.** The average level of conditions in a community or country, or the level of conditions people consider necessary for a happy, satisfying life. In countries with a high standard of living, many different goods and services are considered to be necessities. In countries with a low standard of living, many of these same items are luxuries enjoyed by only a few people.

**Surinam** (sur′ə nam). A partner in the Kingdom of the Netherlands. Located on the northeastern coast of South America. (See map, page 9.) Formerly called Dutch Guiana. See **Kingdom of the Netherlands.**

---

**Syrian** (sir′ē ən). Refers to people from the country of Syria, on the eastern coast of the Mediterranean Sea. Also refers to their descendants.

**tannin.** An acid made from quebracho wood and other plants. One of its uses is for tanning animal hides. See **quebracho.**

**three-dimensional** (də men′shən l). Having height, width, and depth.

**Titicaca** (tit′ə kä′kə), **Lake.** One of the largest lakes in South America, 12,500 feet above sea level. Located on the border between Peru and Bolivia. (See map, page 9.)

**toquilla** (tō kē′yə). A palmlike plant which grows in South America. The leaves of this plant are cut into strips to make Panama hats.

**tributaries.** Streams or rivers that flow into a larger stream or a lake.

**tropical rainforest.** Also called rainforest. A dense forest of trees, vines, and other plants found in the tropics. Yearly rainfall ranges from 60 to over 100 inches. (See vegetation map, page 22.) See **tropics.**

**Tropic of Cancer.** An imaginary line around the earth, about 1,600 miles north of the equator.

**Tropic of Capricorn.** An imaginary line around the earth, about 1,600 miles south of the equator.

**tropics.** The part of the earth on both sides of the equator where the weather is generally hot all year round. Extends from the Tropic of Cancer in the north to the Tropic of Capricorn in the south. Also called the Torrid Zone.

**tungsten** (tung′stən). A grayish white metal. Used in making high-quality steel, wires for electric light bulbs, and other products.

**underdeveloped.** Refers to those countries in which most work is done by the muscle power of men and animals. In underdeveloped countries, many natural resources are poorly used and the standard of living is low.

**United Nations.** An organization formed in 1945 to work for world peace. More than 130 nations are members. Agencies related to the United Nations work to solve problems in fields such as health, agriculture, and labor.

**Uruguay** (yur′ə gwā). One of the smallest countries in South America. Located on the southeastern coast of the continent. (See map, page 9.)

**Valdivia** (väl dē′vyä), **Pedro de,** 1500?-1553. A Spanish soldier. Founded the city of Santiago, Chile, in 1541.

**Venezuela** (ven′ə zwē′lə). A country in the northern part of South America. (See map, page 9.)

**vicuña** (vi kün′yə). A wild animal of the camel family, native to South America. Found in the Andes Mountains of Peru, Ecuador, and Bolivia.

**Villa-Lobos** (vē′lä lō′bôs), **Heitor,** 1884-1959. An outstanding Brazilian composer, conductor, and teacher.

**volcano** (vol kā′nō). An opening in the earth's crust through which molten rock and cinders are forced to the surface. As the hot material cools, it forms a hill or mountain. This mountain or hill is also called a volcano.

**Volta** (väl′tə) **Redonda** (ri dän′də). A city in eastern Brazil. (See map, page 61.) Leading iron and steel center in South America.

**Western Hemisphere.** The half of the world in which the continents of North America and South America are situated.

**World Bank.** Short name commonly used for the International Bank for Reconstruction and Development. It has its headquarters in Washington, D.C. The governments of about 115 countries are members of this bank and contribute money to it. When these nations need money for building highways, constructing dams, or making other improvements, they may borrow it from the World Bank.

**yerba** (yėr′bə) **maté** (mä′tā). An evergreen shrub that grows in South America. Its leaves are used to make a tea called maté.

# INDEX

Explanation of abbreviations used in this Index:

*p* — picture      *m* — map

---

PRONUNCIATION KEY: hat, āge, cãre, fär; let, ēqual, tėrm; it, īce; hot, ōpen, ôrder; oil, out; cup, pu̇t, rüle, ūse; child; long; thin; ᴛнen; zh, measure; ə represents a in about, e in taken, i in pencil, o in lemon, u in circus. For the complete key, see page 137.

PRONUNCIATION KEY: hat, āge, cāre, fär; let, ēqual, tèrm; it, īce; hot, ōpen, ôrder; oil, out; cup, pùt, rüle, ūse; child; long; thin; ҭнen; zh, measure; ə represents a in about, e in taken, i in pencil, o in lemon, u in circus. For the complete key, see page 137.

## List of Maps

# Acknowledgments

Grateful acknowledgment is made to the following for permission to use the illustrations found in this book:

A. Devaney, Inc.: Pages 4-5 and 48

Adrian Beerhorst: Page 32

Alpha Photo Associates, Inc.: Pages 50-51; pages 54-55 by Hamilton Wright

Annan Photo Features: Page 103

Carl Frank: Pages 21, 44, 82-83, 88-89, and 101

Carl E. Östman: Pages 6-7; page 13 of the Skills Manual

Culver Pictures: Pages 34-35

Design Photographers International: Pages 74-75 by Jerry Frank

Erich Hess: Pages 45, 52-53, and 59

Ewing Galloway: Pages 24 and 73

Freelance Photographers Guild: Pages 2-3; page 81 by Peter Gridley; pages 96-97 by Emil Willemetz; pages 130-131 by Herzog; page 2 of the Skills Manual

Hans Mann: Pages 72-73

Magnum Photos, Inc.: Page 57 by Cornell Capa; page 84 by Sergio Larrain

Manchete Press Agency: Pages 65, 76, and 134

Monkmeyer Press Photo Service: Pages 82 and 108

Museu Paulista-São Paulo, Brazil: Page 42, painting by Pedro Americo

Pan American Union: Page 68, painting by Cândido Portinari

Paul Popper, Ltd.: Pages 58 and 93

Peruvian Embassy: Pages 36-37, painting by Rugendas

Photoreporters, Inc.: Page 43 by Santi Visalli

Photo Researchers, Inc.: Pages 70-71 by George Holton; page 92 by Carl Frank; page 99 by Fritz Henle

Publix Pictorial Service Corporation: Pages 10-11 and 16

Rapho Guillumette Pictures: Page 23 by Georg Gerster

Raymond E. Fideler: Page 13

Republic of Venezuela Office of Central Information: Page 116

Shostal Associates, Inc.: Pages 14, 17, 18-19, 26-27, 46-47, 60, 62-63, 66-67, 78-79, 80, 86-87, 94-95, 98, 111, and 132-133

The American Museum of Natural History: Page 29

The Bettmann Archive: Pages 38-39

Varig Brazilian Airlines: Pages 112-113 and 118

Venezuela Ministerio de Informaccion: Pages 40-41

William's Fotostudio: Pages 104-105

Zentrale Farbbild Agentur: Pages 53, 106-107, and 109; pages 30-31 by Janoud. Single edition pages ii-iii

Grateful acknowledgment is made to Scott, Foresman and Company for the pronunciation system used in this book, which is taken from the Thorndike-Barnhart Dictionary Series.

Grateful acknowledgment is made to the following for permission to use cartographic data in this book: Creative Arts: Top maps on page 11 of the Skills Manual; Nystrom Raised Relief Map Company, Chicago 60618: Bottom map on page 11 of the Skills Manual; Rand McNally & Company: Cover and page 1; United States Department of Commerce, Bureau of the Census: Lower left-hand map on page 10 of the Skills Manual.

# SKILLS MANUAL

## CONTENTS

# Thinking and Solving Problems

**Why the social studies are important to you.** During the next few years, you will make an important choice. You will choose whether or not you will direct your own life. Many people are never aware of making this choice. They drift through life, never really trying to understand what is going on around them or why things turn out the way they do. Without knowing it, these people have chosen not to direct their own lives. As a result, they miss many enriching experiences. Other people make a serious effort to choose a way of life that will bring them satisfaction. If you decide to live by choice instead of by chance, you will be able to live a more satisfying life.

You will need three types of knowledge to live by choice successfully. Living by choice will demand a great deal from you. You will have to keep growing

**A laboratory worker in an Argentine textile plant.** Unlike the man shown below, most people who live in South America do not have the skills needed by modern industry. Why is this so? What effect does the lack of skilled workers have on the development of industry in South America? The problem-solving method can help you discover answers to these questions.

# Thinking and the Three Types of Learnings

## THINKING

One of the main reasons you are attending school is to develop your ability to think clearly. Thinking includes seven different thought processes. (See definitions below.) If you learn to use your higher thought processes, rather than simply repeat information you have memorized, you will achieve greater success in school and in life. In fact, your ability to fulfill your obligations as a citizen will depend largely on how well you learn to think. Your ability to think clearly will also help you make progress in the three types of learnings included in the social studies. (See chart below.)

### Seven Thought Processes

1. **Remembering** is recalling or recognizing information.
2. **Translation** is changing information from one form into another, such as words into pictures.
3. **Interpretation** is discovering relationships among facts, concepts,* and generalizations.*
4. **Application** is applying the appropriate knowledge and skills to the solution of a new problem.
5. **Analysis** is separating complicated material into its basic parts to see how those parts were put together, how they are related to each other, and how the parts are related to the whole.
6. **Synthesis** is putting ideas together in a form that is not only meaningful but also new and original.
7. **Evaluation** is judging whether something is acceptable or unacceptable, according to definite standards.

## THREE TYPES OF LEARNINGS

| Understandings | Values and Attitudes | Skills |
|---|---|---|
| Concepts | Beliefs | Obtaining knowledge |
| Generalizations | Appreciations | Using knowledge |
| Facts | Ideals | Working with others |

### Understandings
You will truly gain an understanding of important concepts and generalizations when you use your thought processes to organize information in meaningful ways. In turn, the concepts and generalizations you develop will help you learn to think critically about new situations you meet.

### Values and Attitudes
You will develop many constructive values and attitudes as you improve your thinking ability. Success in the higher levels of thinking will bring you faith that you can solve problems and make wise decisions. In turn, positive values and attitudes will help you to develop your thinking ability.

### Skills
You will be more successful in developing the social studies skills when you use your higher thought processes described above. In turn, you will find that the social studies skills will help you do the critical thinking needed for solving the many difficult problems you will face during your lifetime.

*See Four Words To Understand, page 5

in three different types of learnings — understandings, values and attitudes, and skills. As the chart on page 3 shows, the type of learnings we call understandings includes the kinds of information you need in order to understand yourself, your country, and your world. The type of learnings we call values and attitudes deals with the way you feel toward yourself and your world. The third type of learnings includes the skills you need to use in gaining understandings and developing constructive values and attitudes. Among these skills are those you need for obtaining and using knowledge, and for working effectively with other people.

The social studies can help you grow in the three types of learnings. Your social studies class is one of the best places in which you can explore the three types of learnings. Here you can obtain much of the information you need for understanding yourself and your world. You can practice many important skills. Through many experiences, you can begin to evaluate what in life is worthwhile to you.

**The problem-solving method will help you achieve success in social studies.** Since the social studies are of such great importance, you want to use the best possible study method. You could just read a textbook and memorize answers for a test. If you did so, however, you would forget much of the information soon after the test was over. Your thinking ability would not improve, and you would not gain new, constructive values and attitudes. You would not have the opportunity to use many important skills, either. We suggest that you use a special way of studying called the problem-solving method. You will want

to use the problem-solving method as you do research. To use this method, follow these steps.

**1. Do some general background reading** in this book about a topic such as land, people, natural resources, or industry.

**2. Choose an important, interesting problem** that you would like to solve. Write it down so that you will have clearly in mind what it is you want to find out. (Look at the sample problem on page 5.) If there are small problems that need to be solved in order to solve your big problem, list them, too.

**3. Consider all possible solutions to your problem** and list the ones that seem most likely to be true. These possible solutions are called "educated guesses," or hypotheses. You will try to solve your problem by finding facts to support or disprove your hypotheses.

**4. Test your hypotheses** by doing research. This book provides you with four main sources of information. These are the pictures, the text, the maps, and the Glossary. To locate the information you need, you may use the Table of Contents and the Index. The suggestions on pages 13-17 of this Skills Manual will help you to locate and evaluate other sources of information.

As you do research, make notes of all the information you find that will either support your hypotheses or disprove them. You may discover that information from one source disagrees with information from another. If this should happen, check still further and try to decide which facts are correct.

**5. Summarize what you have learned.** Have you been able to support one or more of your hypotheses with facts? Have you been able to disprove one or more of your hypotheses? What new facts have you learned? Do you need to do further research?

You may want to write a report about the problem. To help other people share the ideas that you have come to understand, you may decide to illustrate your research project with maps, pictures, or your own drawings. You will find helpful suggestions for writing a good report on pages 17 and 18 of this Skills Manual.

**You can use the problem-solving method throughout your life.** In addition to helping you to achieve success in the social studies, the problem-solving method can help you in another way. By using it, you will learn to deal with problems in a way that will be valuable to you throughout your life. Many successful scientists, businessmen, and government leaders use this method to solve problems.

**A sample problem to solve.** As you make discoveries about South America, you may wish to investigate problems about the continent as a whole or about one South American country. The following sample problem is about the continent as a whole.

Climate in South America varies greatly from one part of the continent to another. How does climate in South America affect the people who live there? In order to solve this problem, you will need to make several hypotheses about the ways in which the different climates affect the people. The following questions suggest some hypotheses.

1. What facts about differences in rainfall from place to place in South America help to solve this problem?
2. What facts about differences in temperature help to solve it?
3. What facts about farming in South America help to solve it?

## Four Words To Understand

1. **A concept** is a big, general idea that includes many smaller, more specific ideas. An example of a concept is the idea of "trade." Many kinds of exchange are included in this idea. Two boys who exchange marbles on the playground are carrying on trade. A woman who pays money to the grocer for a loaf of bread is also carrying on trade; so is a factory that buys raw materials from other countries and sells its manufactured products overseas. Only as you come to see the various things that the word "trade" includes do you grow to understand this concept. Another example of a concept is the idea of "climate."

2. **A generalization** is a general rule or principle that expresses a meaningful relationship among two or more concepts. It is formed by drawing a conclusion from a group of facts. For example, "Through trade, all people on the earth can have a better living," is a generalization drawn from facts about trade and the way people live in various parts of the world. It includes four concepts: "trade," "all people," "the earth," and "a better living." These have been put together to give a significant understanding about the world. The many facts you read about, hear about, or experience will make more sense if you think of them as statements that can be combined to form meaningful generalizations. Remember, however, that if a generalization is based on wrong or insufficient facts, or is carelessly thought out, it may be false. Make certain that you understand the concepts in a generalization, and judge carefully whether or not you think it is true.

3. **Values** are the things in life that a person considers right, desirable, or worthwhile. For instance, if you believe that every individual is important, we may say that one of your values is the worth of the individual.

4. **Attitudes** are the outward expression of a person's values. For example, a person who truly values the worth of every individual will express this value by treating everyone he meets with consideration.

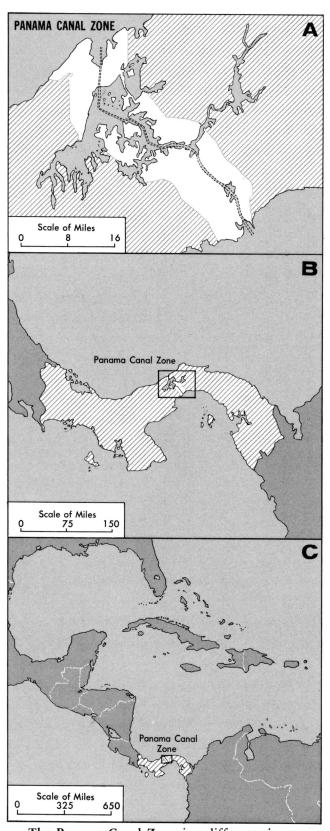

PANAMA CANAL ZONE

**A**

Scale of Miles
0    8    16

**B**

Panama Canal Zone

Scale of Miles
0    75    150

**C**

Panama Canal Zone

Scale of Miles
0    325    650

The Panama Canal Zone is a different size on each of the three maps above. This is because one inch on each of these maps represents a different distance on the surface of the earth.

# Learning Map Skills

**The earth is a sphere.** Our earth is round like a ball. We call any object with this shape a sphere. The earth is, of course, a very large sphere. Its diameter* is about 8,000 miles. Its circumference* is about 25,000 miles. The earth is not quite a perfect sphere, however, for it is slightly flattened at the North and South poles.

**Globes and maps.** The globe in your classroom is also a sphere. It is a model of the earth. The surface of the globe shows the shapes of the landmasses and bodies of water on the earth. By looking at the globe, you can see exactly where the continents, islands, and oceans are located. Globes are made with the North Pole at the top, but they are usually tilted to represent the way that the earth is tilted. Maps are flat drawings that represent part or all of the earth's surface.

**Scale.** Globes and maps give information about distance. When you use them, you need to know how many miles on the earth are represented by a given distance on the globe or map. This relationship is called the scale. The scale of a globe or map may be expressed in several different ways.

On most maps, the scale is shown by a small drawing. For example:

Scale of Miles    0    200    400

Sometimes, the scale is expressed in this way: 1 inch = 400 miles.

Scale is often shown in another way, especially on globes and large maps. For example: 1:10,000,000. These numbers mean that any given distance on the globe or map represents a distance on the earth that is ten million times as large. When the scale is shown in this way, you may use any kind of measuring unit you wish. If you choose the inch, then one inch on the globe or map equals ten million inches on the earth, or about 158 miles. You might, however, prefer to use the centimeter,* another measuring unit. In that case, one centimeter on the globe or map would represent ten million centimeters on the earth, or 100 kilometers.

*See Glossary

**Locating places on the earth.** Map makers, travelers, and other curious people have always wanted to know just where certain places are located. Over the years, a very accurate way of giving such information has been worked out. This system is used all over the world.

In order to work out a system for locating anything, you need starting points and a measuring unit. The North and South poles and the equator are the starting points for the system we use to locate places on the earth. The measuring unit for our system is called the degree (°).

**Parallels show latitude.** When we want to locate a place on the earth, we first find out how far it is north or south of the equator. This distance measured in degrees is called north or south latitude. The equator represents zero latitude. The North Pole is located at 90 degrees north latitude, and the South Pole is at 90 degrees south latitude.

All points on the earth that have the same latitude are the same distance from the equator. A line connecting such points is called a parallel. This is because it is parallel to the equator. (See illustration D, below.)

**Meridians show longitude.** After we know the latitude of a place, we need to know its location in an east-west direction. This is called its longitude. The lines that show longitude are called meridians. They are drawn so as to connect the North and South poles. (See illustration E, below.) Longitude is measured from the meridian that passes through Greenwich, England. This line of zero longitude is called the prime meridian. Distance east or west of this meridian measured in degrees is called east or west longitude. The meridian of 180 degrees west longitude is the same as the one of 180 degrees east longitude. This is because 180 degrees is exactly halfway around the world from the prime meridian.

**Locating places on a globe.** The location of a certain place might be given to you like this: 30°N 90°W. This means that this place is located 30 degrees north of the equator, and 90 degrees west of the prime meridian. See if you can find this place on the globe in your classroom. It is helpful to remember that parallels and meridians are drawn every ten or fifteen degrees on most globes.

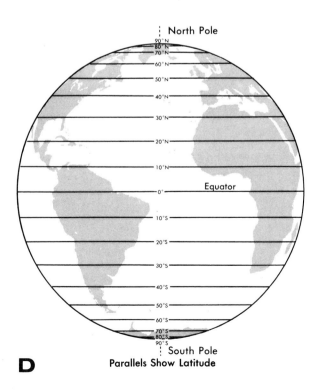

**D**
**Parallels Show Latitude**

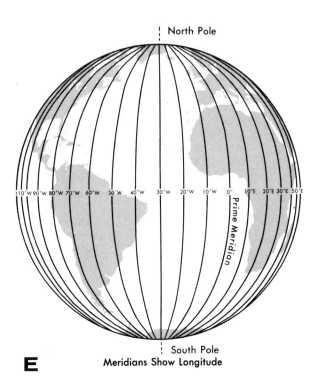

**E**
**Meridians Show Longitude**

**The round earth on a flat map.** An important fact about a sphere is that you cannot flatten out its surface perfectly. To prove this, you might perform an experiment. Cut an orange in half and scrape away the fruit. You will not be able to press either piece of orange peel flat without crushing it. If you cut one piece in half, however, you can press these smaller pieces nearly flat. Next, cut one of these pieces of peel into three sections, or gores, shaped like those in illustration F, below. You will be able to press these small sections quite flat.

A map like the one shown in illustration F can be made by cutting the surface of a globe into twelve pieces shaped like the smallest sections of your orange peel. Such

a map would be fairly accurate. However, an "orange-peel" map is not an easy map to use, because the continents and oceans are split apart.

A flat map can never show the earth's surface as truthfully as a globe can. On globes, shape, size, distance, and direction are all accurate. Although a single flat map of the world cannot be drawn to show all four of these things correctly, flat maps can be made that show some of these things accurately. The various ways of drawing maps of the world to show different things correctly are called map projections.

**The Mercator\* projection.** Illustration G, below, shows a world map called a Mercator projection. When you compare this map

## A Round Globe on a Flat Surface

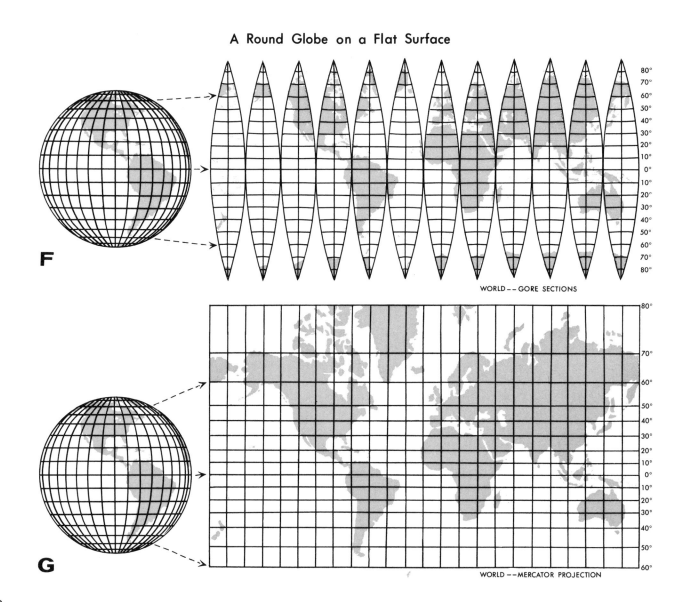

WORLD -- GORE SECTIONS

WORLD --MERCATOR PROJECTION

8

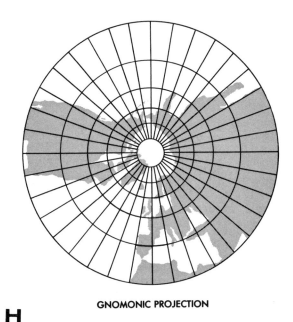

GNOMONIC PROJECTION

H

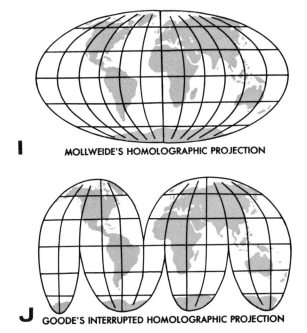

I MOLLWEIDE'S HOMOLOGRAPHIC PROJECTION

J GOODE'S INTERRUPTED HOMOLOGRAPHIC PROJECTION

with a globe, you can see that continents, islands, and oceans have almost the right shape. On this kind of map, however, North America seems larger than Africa, which is not true. On Mercator maps, lands far from the equator appear larger than they are.

Because they show true directions, Mercator maps are especially useful to navigators. For instance, the city of Lisbon, Portugal, lies almost exactly east of Baltimore, Maryland. A Mercator map shows that a ship could reach Lisbon by sailing from Baltimore straight east across the Atlantic Ocean.

**The shortest route.** Strangely enough, the best way to reach Lisbon from Baltimore is not by traveling straight east. There is a shorter route. In order to understand why this is so, you might like to perform the following experiment.

On your classroom globe, locate Lisbon and Baltimore. Both cities lie just south of the 40th parallel. Take a piece of string and connect the two cities. Let the string follow the true east-west direction of the 40th parallel. Now, draw the string tight. Notice that it passes far to the north of the 40th parallel. The path of the tightened string is the shortest route between Baltimore and Lisbon. The shortest route between any two points on the earth is called the great* circle route.

**The gnomonic (nō mon′ ik) projection.** Using a globe and a piece of string is not a very handy or accurate way of finding great circle routes. Instead, sailors and fliers use a special kind of map called the gnomonic projection. (See illustration H, above.) On this kind of map, the great circle route between any two places can be found simply by drawing a straight line between them.

**Equal-area projections.** Mercator and gnomonic maps are both very useful, but they do not show true areas. They cannot be used when you want to compare areas in different parts of the world. This is because sections of these maps that are the same size do not always represent the same amounts of the earth's surface.

Maps that do show true areas are called equal-area projections. If one square*inch of such a map represents a certain number of square miles on the earth's surface, then every other square inch of the map will represent an equal number of square miles on the earth. In order to draw an equal-area map of the world on a flat surface, the shapes of the landmasses and bodies of water must be distorted. (See illustration I, above.) To avoid this, some equal-area maps are broken, or interrupted. The breaks are arranged to fall at places that are not important. (See illustration J, above.)

## SPECIAL-PURPOSE MAPS

**Maps that show part of the earth.** For some purposes, we prefer maps that do not show the entire surface of the earth. A map of a very small area can be drawn more accurately than a map of a large area. It can also include more details.

Illustration K, below, shows a photograph and a map of the same small part of the earth. The drawings on the map that show the shape and location of things on the earth are called symbols. The small drawing that shows directions is called a compass* rose.

**Maps for special purposes.** Maps can show the location of many different kinds of things. For instance, a map can show what minerals are found in certain places, or what crops are grown. A small chart that lists the symbols and their meanings is usually included on a map. This is called the legend, or key. (See map M, below.)

Symbols on some geography maps stand for the amounts of things in different places. For instance, map L, below, gives information about the number of people in the western part of the United States. The key tells the meaning of the symbols, which in this case are dots and circles.

On different maps, the same symbol may stand for different things and amounts. For example, each dot on map L stands for 10,000 persons. On other maps, a dot might represent 5,000 sheep or 1,000 bushels of wheat.

There are other ways of giving information about quantity. For example, various designs or patterns may be used on a rainfall map to indicate the areas that receive different amounts of rain each year.

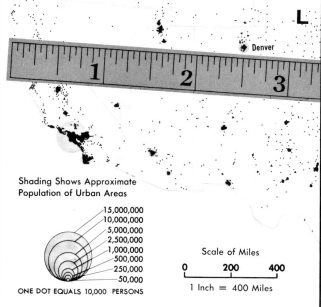

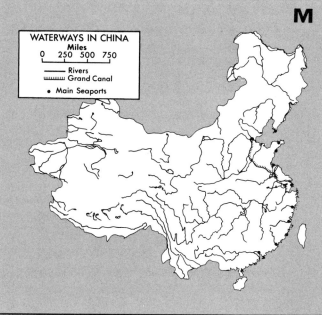

## RELIEF MAPS

**Some globes and maps show the roughness of the earth's surface.** From a jet plane, you can see that the earth's surface is irregular. You can see mountains and valleys, hills and plains. For some purposes, globes and maps that show these things are needed. They are called relief globes and maps.

Since globes are three-dimensional models of the earth, you may wonder why most globes do not show the roughness of the earth's surface. The reason for this is that the highest mountain on the earth is not very large when it is compared with the earth's diameter. Even a very large globe would be almost perfectly smooth.

In order to make a relief globe or map, you must use a different scale for the height of the land. For example, you might start with a large flat map. One inch on your flat map represents a distance of one hundred miles on the earth. Now you are going to make a model of a mountain on your map. On the earth, this mountain is two miles high. If you let one inch represent a height of two miles on the earth, your mountain should rise one inch above the flat surface of

your map. Other mountains and hills should be modeled on this same scale.

By photographing relief globes and maps, flat maps can be made that show the earth much as it looks from an airplane. Maps N and O, at the top of this page, are photographs of a relief globe. Map P is a photograph of a relief map.

**Topographic maps.** Another kind of map that shows the roughness of the earth's surface is called a topographic, or contour, map. On this kind of map, lines are drawn to show

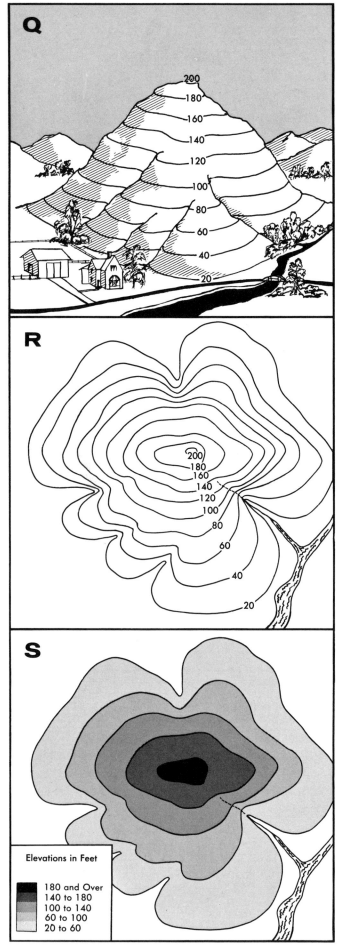

**Q**

**R**

**S**

Elevations in Feet

180 and Over
140 to 180
100 to 140
60 to 100
20 to 60

different heights of the earth's surface. These are called contour lines. The illustrations on this page help to explain how topographic maps are made.

Illustration Q is a drawing of a hill. Around the bottom of the hill is our first contour line. This line connects all the points at the base of the hill that are exactly twenty feet above sea level. Higher up the hill, another contour line is drawn, connecting all the points that are exactly forty feet above sea level. A line is also drawn at a height of sixty feet. Other lines are drawn every twenty feet until the top of the hill is reached. Since the hill is shaped somewhat like a cone, each contour line is shorter than the one just below it.

Illustration R shows how the contour lines in the drawing of the hill (Q) can be used to make a topographic map. This map gives us a great deal of information about the hill. Since each line is labeled with the height it represents, you can tell how high the different parts of the hill are. It is important to remember that land does not really rise in layers, as you might think when you look at a topographic map. Wherever the contour lines are far apart, you can be sure that the land slopes gently. Where they are close together, the slope is steep. With practice, you can picture the land in your mind as you look at such a map. Topographic maps are especially useful to men who design such things as roads and buildings.

On a topographic map, the spaces between the contour lines may be filled in with different shades of gray. If a different shade of gray were used for each different height of land shown in map R, there would be ten shades. It would be very hard for you to tell these different shades of gray apart. Therefore, on map S, at left, black and four shades of gray were used to show differences in height of forty feet. The key box shows the height of the land represented by the different shades. On some topographic maps, colors are used to represent different heights of land.

Children attending an open-air school in Peru. What skills do you think these children are learning?

## Learning Social Studies Skills

**What is a skill?** A skill is something that you have learned to do well. To learn some skills, such as swimming, you must train the muscles of your arms and legs. To learn others, such as typing, you must train your fingers. Still other skills require you to train your mind. For example, reading with understanding is a skill that requires much mental training. The skills that you use in the social studies are largely mental skills.

**Why are skills important?** Mastering different skills will help you to have a more satisfying life. You will be healthier and enjoy your leisure time more if you develop skills needed to take part in various sports. By developing artistic skills, you will be able to express your feelings more fully. It is even more important for you to develop skills of the mind. These skills are the tools that you will use in obtaining and using the knowledge you need to live successfully in today's world.

**To develop a skill, you must practice it correctly.** If you ask a fine athlete or musician how he gained his skill, he will say, "Through practice." To develop skills of the mind, you must practice also. Remember, however, that a person cannot become a good ballplayer if he keeps throwing the ball incorrectly. The same thing is true of mental skills. To master them, you must practice them correctly.

The following pages contain suggestions about how to perform correctly several important skills needed in the social studies. Study these skills carefully, and use them.

### How To Find Information You Need

Each day of your life you seek information. Sometimes you want to know certain facts just because you are curious. Most of the time, however, you want information for some special purpose. If your hobby is baseball, for example, you may want to know how to figure batting averages. If you collect stamps, you need to know how to identify the countries they come from. As a student in today's world, you need information for many purposes. As an adult, you will need even more knowledge to live successfully in tomorrow's world.

You may wonder how you can possibly learn all the facts you are going to need during your lifetime. The answer is that you can't. Therefore, knowing how to find information when you need it is of vital importance to you. Following are suggestions for locating good sources of information and for using these sources to find the facts that you need.

**Written Sources of Information**

1. <u>Books</u>. You may be able to find the information you need in books that you have at home or in your classroom. To see if a textbook or other nonfiction book has the information you need, look at the table of contents and the index.

Sometimes, you will need to go to your school or community library to locate books that contain the information you want. To make the best use of a library, you should learn to use the card catalog. This is a file that contains information about the books in the library. Each nonfiction book has at least three cards, filed in alphabetical order. One is for the title, one is for the author, and one is for the subject of the book. Each card gives the book's special number. This number will help you to find the book, since all the nonfiction books in the library are arranged on the shelves in numerical order. If you cannot find a book you want, the librarian will be glad to help you.

2. <u>Reference volumes</u>. You will find much useful information in special books known as reference volumes. These include dictionaries, encyclopedias, atlases, and other special books. Some companies publish a book each year with statistics and general information about the events of the preceding year. Such books are usually called yearbooks, annuals, or almanacs.

3. <u>Newspapers and magazines</u>. These are important sources of up-to-date information. Sometimes you will want to look for information in papers or magazines that you do not have at home. You can usually find the ones you want at the library.

The *Readers' Guide to Periodical Literature,* which is available in most libraries, will direct you to magazine articles about the subject you are investigating. This is a series of volumes that list articles by title, author, and subject. In the front of each volume is an explanation of the abbreviations used to indicate the different magazines and their dates.

4. <u>Booklets, pamphlets, and bulletins</u>. Many materials of this type are available from local and state governments, as well as from our federal government. Chambers of commerce, travel bureaus, trade organizations, private companies, and embassies of foreign countries publish materials that contain a wealth of information.

Many booklets and bulletins give accurate information. You should remember, however, that some of them are intended to promote certain products or ideas. Information obtained from such sources should be checked carefully.

**Reading for Information**

The following suggestions will help you to save time and effort when you are looking for information in books and other written materials.

1. <u>Use the table of contents and the index</u>. The table of contents appears at the beginning of the book and generally is a list of the chapters in the book. By looking at this list, you can usually tell whether the book has the type of information you need.

The index is a more detailed list of the topics that are discussed in the book. It will help you locate the pages on which specific facts are discussed. In most books, the index is at the back. Encyclopedias often include the index in a separate volume, however.

At the beginning of an index, you will usually find an explanation that makes it easier to use. For example, the explanation at the beginning of the Index for *South America* tells you that *p* means picture and *m* means map.

The topics, or entries, in the index are arranged in alphabetical order. To locate all the information you need, you may have to look under more than one entry. For example, to find out what pages in this book discuss Indians, look up the entry for Indians. Also, look up the entry for a specific group of Indians, such as the Incas.

2. Skim the written material to see if it contains the information you need. Before you begin reading a chapter or a page, skim it to see if it has the information you need. In this way you will not run the risk of wasting time reading something that is of little or no value to you. When you skim, you look mainly for topic headings, topic sentences, and key words. For example, imagine you are looking for the answer to the question: "Why is São Paulo, Brazil, an important industrial city?" In the Industry chapter of *South America*, you might look for a topic heading that mentions industrial cities. When you find this topic heading, you might look for a key term such as "São Paulo."

3. Read carefully when you think you have located the information you need. When you think you have found the page that contains the information you are looking for, read it carefully. Does it really tell you what you want to know? If not, you will need to look further.

**Other Ways of Obtaining Information**

1. Direct experience. What you observe or experience for yourself may be a good source of information if you have observed carefully and remembered accurately. First-hand information can often be obtained by visiting places in your community or nearby, such as museums, factories, or government offices.

2. Radio and television. Use the listings in your local newspaper to find programs about the subjects in which you are interested.

3. Movies, filmstrips, recordings, and slides. Materials on a great variety of subjects are available. They can be obtained from schools, libraries, museums, and private companies.

4. Resource people. Sometimes, you will be able to obtain information by interviewing a person who has special knowledge. On occasion, you may wish to invite someone to speak to your class and answer questions.

## Evaluating Information

During your lifetime, you will constantly need to evaluate what you see, hear, and read. Information is not true or significant simply because it is presented on television or is written in a book, magazine, or newspaper. The following suggestions will help you in evaluating information.

**Learn to tell the difference between primary and secondary sources of information.** A primary source of information is a firsthand record. For example, a photograph taken of an event while it is happening is a primary source. So is the report you write about a field trip you take. Original documents, such as the Constitution of the United States, are primary sources, also.

A secondary source is a secondhand report. For example, if you write a report about what someone else told you he saw, your report will be a secondary source of information. Another example of a secondary source is a history book.

Advanced scholars like to use primary sources whenever possible. However, these sources are often difficult to obtain. Most students in elementary and high school use secondary sources. You should always be aware that you are using secondhand information when you use a secondary source.

**Find out who said it and when it was said.** The next step in evaluating information is to ask, "Who said it?" Was he a scholar with special training in the subject about which he wrote? Was he a newsman with a reputation for careful reporting of the facts?

Another question you should ask is, "When was it said?" Changes take place rapidly in our world, and the information you are using may be out of date. For example, many nations in Africa have won independence in recent years, so a political map of this continent that is ten years old is no longer accurate.

**Find out if it is mainly fact or opinion.** The next step in evaluating information is to decide whether it is based on facts or whether it mainly consists of unsupported opinions. You can do this best if you are aware of these three types of statements.

1. Statements of fact that can be checked. For example, "Voters in the United States choose their representatives by secret ballot " is a statement of fact that can be checked by observing how voting is carried on in different parts of our country.

2. Inferences, or conclusions that are based on facts. The statement "The people of the United States live in a democracy " is an inference. This inference is based on the fact that the citizens choose their representatives by secret ballot, and on other facts that can be proved. It is important to remember that inferences can be false or only partly true.

3. Value judgments, or opinions. The statement "It is always wrong for a country to go to war " is a value judgment. Since a value judgment is an opinion,

you need to examine it very critically. On what facts and inferences is it based? For example, what facts and conclusions do you think form the basis of the opinion: "It is always wrong for a country to go to war"? Do you agree or disagree with these conclusions? A reliable writer or reporter is careful to let his reader know which statements in his writing are his own opinions. He also tries to base his opinions as much as possible on facts that can be proved.

**Find out why it was said.** The next step in evaluating information is to find out the purpose for which it was prepared. Many books and articles are prepared in an honest effort to give you accurate information. For example, a scientist writing about a new scientific discovery will usually try to report his findings as accurately as possible, and he will be careful to distinguish between what he has actually observed and the conclusions he has drawn from these facts.

Some information, however, is prepared mainly to persuade people to believe or act a certain way. Information of this kind is called propaganda.

Some propaganda is used to promote causes that are generally considered good. A picture that shows Smokey the Bear and the words "Only *you* can prevent forest fires" is an example of this kind of propaganda.

Propaganda is also used to make people support causes they would not agree with if they knew more about them. This kind of propaganda may consist of information that is true, partly true, or false. Even when it is true, however, the information may be presented in such a way as to mislead you.

Propaganda generally appeals to people's emotions rather than to their reasoning ability. For this reason, you should learn to identify information that is propaganda. Then you can think about it calmly and clearly, and evaluate it intelligently.

# Seven Propaganda Tricks

People who use propaganda have learned many ways of presenting information to influence you in the direction they wish. Seven propaganda tricks to watch for are listed below.

**Name Calling.** Giving a label that is disliked or feared, such as "un-American," to an organization, a person, or an idea. This trick often persuades people to reject something they know nothing about.

**Glittering Generalities.** Trying to win support by using fine-sounding phrases, such as "the best deal in town," or "the American way." These phrases have no clear meaning when you stop and think about them.

**Transfer.** Connecting a person, product, or idea with something that people already feel strongly about. For example, displaying a picture of a church next to a speaker to give the impression that he is honest and trustworthy.

**Testimonial.** Getting well-known persons or organizations to announce in public their support of a person, product, or idea.

**Plain Folks.** Trying to win support by giving the impression of being just an ordinary person who can be trusted. For example, a political candidate may try to win people's confidence by giving the impression that he is a good father who loves children and dogs.

**Card Stacking.** Giving the wrong impression by giving only part of the facts about a person, product, or idea. For example, giving favorable facts, and leaving out unfavorable ones.

**Bandwagon.** Trying to win support by saying that "everybody knows that," or "everyone is doing this."

---

## Making Reports

There are many occasions when you need to share information or ideas with others. Sometimes you will need to do this in writing. Other times you will need to do it orally. One of the best ways to develop your writing and speaking skills is by making oral and written reports. The success of your report will depend on how well you have organized your material. It will also depend on your skill in presenting it. Here are some guidelines that will help you in preparing a good report.

**Decide upon a goal.** Have your purpose clearly in mind. Are you mainly interested in communicating information? Do you want to give your own viewpoint on a subject, or are you trying to persuade other people to agree with you?

**Find the information you need.** Be sure to use more than one source. If you are not sure how to locate information about your topic, read the suggestions on pages 13-15 of this Skills Manual.

**Take good notes.** To remember what you have read, you must take notes. Before you begin taking notes, however, you will need to make a list of the questions you want your report to answer. As you do research, write down the facts that answer these questions. You may find some interesting and important facts that do not answer any of your questions. If you feel that they might be useful in your report, write them down, too. Your notes should be brief and in your own words except when you want to use exact quotations. When you use a quotation, be sure to put quotation marks around it.

You will be able to make the best use of your notes if you write them on file cards. Use a separate card for each statement or group of statements that answers one of your questions. To remember where your information came from, write on each card the title, author, and date of the source. When you have finished taking notes, group the cards according to the questions they answer. This will help you arrange your material in logical order.

**Make an outline.** After you have reviewed your notes, make an outline. This is a general plan that shows the order and the relationship of the ideas you want to include in your report. The first step in making an outline is to pick out the main ideas. These will be the main headings in your outline. (See sample outline below.) Next, list under each of these headings the ideas and facts that support or explain it. These related ideas are called subheadings. As you arrange your information, ask yourself the following questions.

a. Is there one main idea that I must put first because everything else depends on it?

b. Have I arranged my facts in such a way as to show relationships among them?

c. Are there some ideas that will be clearer if they are discussed after other ideas have been explained?

d. Have I included enough facts so that I can complete my outline with a summary statement or a logical conclusion?

When you have completed your first outline, you may find that some parts of it are skimpy. If so, you may wish to do more research. When you are satisfied that you have enough information, make your final outline. Remember that this outline will serve as the basis of your finished report.

**Example of an outline.** The author of this feature prepared the following outline before writing "Making Reports."

    I.   Introduction
   II.  Deciding upon a goal
  III.  Finding information
  IV.  Taking notes
      A.  List main ideas to be researched
      B.  Write on file cards facts that support or explain these ideas
      C.  Group cards according to main ideas
   V.  Making an outline
      A.  Purpose of an outline
      B.  Guidelines for arranging information
      C.  Sample outline of this section
  VI.  Preparing a written report
 VII.  Presenting an oral report

**Special guidelines for a written report.** As a guide in writing your report, use the outline you have prepared. The following suggestions will help you to make your report interesting and clear.

Create word pictures that your readers can see in their minds. Before you begin to write, imagine that you are going to make a movie of the subject you plan to write about. What scenes would you like to show on the screen? Next, think of the words that will create these same pictures in your readers' minds.

Group your sentences into good paragraphs. It is usually best to begin a paragraph with a topic sentence that says to the reader, "This is what you will learn about in this paragraph." The other sentences in the paragraph should help to support or explain the topic sentence.

A sample paragraph. Below is a sample paragraph from this book. The topic sentence has been underlined. Notice how clear it is and how well the other sentences support it. Also notice how many pictures the paragraph puts in your mind.

> The Incas built excellent roads to connect the different parts of the empire. A stone road extended through the Andes from what is now Quito, Ecuador, southward through Cuzco and into the central part of what is now Chile. Another road, made of sunbaked clay, stretched along the coast from northern Peru to the central part of Chile. Each of these main highways was from fifteen to twenty-five feet wide. The road through the Andes was an engineering marvel. It ran over stony plateaus and snow-covered ridges. In some places it was more than sixteen thousand feet above the level of the sea.

Other guidelines. There are two other things to remember in writing a good report. First, use the dictionary to find the spelling of words you are doubtful about. Second, make a list of the sources of information you used, and include it at the beginning or end of your report. This list is called a bibliography.

**Special guidelines for an oral report.** When you are going to give a report orally, you will also want to organize your information in a logical order by making an outline. Prepare notes to guide you during your talk. These notes should be complete enough to help you remember all the points you want to make. You may even write out portions of your report that you prefer to read.

When you present your report, speak directly to your audience. Pronounce your words correctly and distinctly. Remember to speak slowly enough for your listeners to follow what you are saying, and use a tone of voice that will hold their interest. Stand up straight, but try not to be too stiff. The only way to improve your speaking skills is to practice them correctly.

### Holding a Group Discussion

One of the important ways in which you learn is by exchanging ideas with other people. You do this frequently in informal conversation. You are likely to learn more, however, when you take part in the special kind of group conversation that we call a discussion. A discussion is more orderly than a conversation, and it usually has a definite, serious purpose. This purpose may be the sharing of information or the solving of a problem. In order to reach its goal, the discussion group must arrive at a conclusion or make a decision of some kind.

A discussion is more likely to be successful when those who take part in it observe the following guidelines.

**1. Be prepared.** Think about the topic to be discussed ahead of time. Prepare for the discussion by reading and taking notes. You may also want to make an outline of the ideas you want to share with the group.

**2. Take part.** Contribute to the discussion; express your ideas clearly and concisely. Be sure that the statements you make and the questions you ask deal with the topic being discussed.

**3. Listen and think.** Listen thoughtfully to others. Encourage all of the members of the discussion group to express their ideas.

## How To Listen

Listening is one of our most valuable communication skills. Each day, we spend a large part of our time listening and speaking to other people face to face. Often, we understand more when we listen to another person speak than we do when we read something he has written. When we listen, we have the advantage of being able to watch his facial expressions and gestures. The following suggestions will help you develop your listening skill.

**Watch the speaker.** As you listen, look directly at the person who is speaking. If you take a sincere interest in what he is saying, you will hear more and learn more. Showing a sincere interest in what the speaker is saying is also an act of courtesy.

**Think about the speaker's message.** Consider carefully what the speaker is saying. Good listening depends mainly on the amount of thinking you do as you listen. Even when you are listening to a well-known lecturer, think about his message as though you were carrying on a personal conversation. If you disagree with something he says, remember the point for later discussion.

**Learn to "picture-listen."** One of the best ways to understand what a speaker is saying is to "picture-listen." When you picture-listen, you see, hear, taste, and smell in your mind the things that the speaker's words describe. These mental images make the words more meaningful.

**Make a list of main images.** As you listen, try to decide which images are the most important. Often, you will want to take notes. Your notes should include all of the main images and facts you wish to remember for a report, a discussion, or some other project.

Do not make up your mind about a question or a problem until all of the facts have been given.

**4. Be courteous.** When you speak, address the entire group. Ask and answer questions politely. When you disagree with someone, point out your reasons calmly and in a friendly way.

### Working With Others

In school and throughout life, you will find that there are many projects that can be done better by a group than by one person working alone. Some of these projects would take too long to finish if they were done by a single individual. Others have different parts that can be done best by people with different talents.

Before your group begins a project, you should decide several matters. First, determine exactly what you are trying to accomplish. Second, decide what part of the project each person should do. Third, schedule when the project is to be completed.

The group will do a better job and reach its goals more quickly if each person follows these suggestions.

**1. Do your part.** Remember that the success of your project depends on every member of the group. Be willing to do your share of the work and to accept your share of the responsibility.

**2. Follow the rules.** Help the group decide on sensible rules, and then follow them. When a difference of opinion cannot be settled by discussion, make a decision by majority vote.

**3. Share your ideas.** Be willing to share your ideas and talents with the group. When you submit an idea for discussion, be prepared to see it criticized or even rejected. At the same time, have the courage to stick up for a principle or a belief that is really important to you.

**4. Respect others.** Remember that every person is an individual with different beliefs and talents. Give the other members of the group a chance to be heard, and be ready to appreciate their work and ideas.

**5. Be friendly, thoughtful, helpful, and cheerful.** Try to express your opinions seriously and sincerely without hurting others or losing their respect. Listen politely to the ideas of others.

**6. Learn from your mistakes.** Look for ways in which you can be a better group member the next time you work with others on a project.

### Building Your Vocabulary

When you do research in many different types of reading materials, you are likely to find several words you have never seen before. If you skip over these words, the chances are that you will not fully understand what you are reading. The following suggestions will help you to discover the meanings of new words and build your vocabulary.

**1. See how the word is used in the sentence.** When you come to a new word, don't stop reading. Read on beyond the new word to see if you can discover any clues to what its meaning might be. Trying to figure out the meaning of a word from the way it is used may not give you the exact definition. However, it will give you a general idea of what the word means.

**2. Sound out the word.** Break the word up into syllables, and try to pronounce it. When you say the word aloud, you may find that you know it after all but have simply never seen it in print.

**3. Look in the dictionary.** When you think you have figured out what a word means and how it is pronounced, check with the dictionary. Have you pronounced it correctly? Did you decide upon the right definition? Remember, most words have several meanings. Do you know which meaning should be used?

**4. Make a list of the new words you learn.** In your own words, write a definition of each word you include in your list. Review this list from time to time.